Molly Wilcox

how much more?

FINDING FULFILLMENT IN A GENEROUS GOD

How Much More? —Copyright ©2022 by Molly Wilcox
Published by UNITED HOUSE Publishing

All rights reserved. No portion of this book may be reproduced or shared in any form–electronic, printed, photocopied, recording, or by any information storage and retrieval system, without prior written permission from the publisher. The use of short quotations is permitted.

Scripture taken from The Message. Copyright © 1993, 1994, 1995, 1996, 2000, 2001, 2002. Used by permission of NavPress Publishing Group.

THE HOLY BIBLE, NEW INTERNATIONAL VERSION®, NIV® Copyright © 1973, 1978, 1984, 2011 by Biblica, Inc.™ Used by permission. All rights reserved worldwide.

Scripture taken from the New King James Version®. Copyright © 1982 by Thomas Nelson, Inc. Used by permission. All rights reserved.

Scripture quotations are from The Holy Bible, English Standard Version® (ESV®), copyright © 2001 by Crossway, a publishing ministry of Good News Publishers. Used by permission. All rights reserved.

Scripture taken from The Voice™. Copyright © 2012 by Ecclesia Bible Society. Used by permission. All rights reserved.

ISBN: 978-1-952840-25-8

UNITED HOUSE Publishing
Waterford, Michigan
info@unitedhousepublishing.com
www.unitedhousepublishing.com

Interior design:
Matt Russell, Marketing Image, mrussell@marketing-image.com

Printed in the United States of America
2022—First Edition

SPECIAL SALES
Most UNITED HOUSE books are available at special quantity discounts when purchased in bulk by corporations, organizations, and special-interest groups. For information, please e-mail orders@unitedhousepublishing.com

*To the girl with the big, crazy God-given dream:
"May He grant the dreams of your heart and see
your plans through to the end." (Psalm 20:4 VOICE)*

"The conversation we need to be having! Where big dreams and deep fulfillment meet to remind us what really matters."

–Hannah Hughes, author, and host of The By Words Show

"Molly leads her readers, not as an overarching authority but as a loving friend. Lending her audience to feeling belonging, and hope. Molly's love for God is infectious and just what I need when I'm weary. Finding *How Much More?* in your hand will not leave you disappointed."

Elisabeth Bennett, Author + Enneagram Coach

"Molly does a beautiful job of putting words to feelings we've all felt that we oftentimes can't articulate. I love that she reminds the reader throughout the entire book that everything the Lord takes us through is ultimately so we grow in deeper dependence and relationship with Him."

-Chelsey DeMatteis, author of *More of Him, Less of Me: Living a Christ-centered Life in a Me-centered World*

"Do I matter? What is my purpose? Where do these longings in my heart come from? Molly Wilcox delves into each of these questions and more in her new book, *How Much More?* Not only does she thoughtfully consider such questions, but she does so as an encouraging friend who has wrestled with them herself and found the answer. In each chapter, Molly helps you discover the hope, fulfillment, and inspiration that already lives in you through Christ. Join Molly to uncover the greatest joy of living your life on purpose - God's purpose for your life and His Kingdom."

- Tina Reale, author of Come and See: *Pursuing Christ's Presence and the Power of the Gospel In Your Everyday Life*

"I believe there comes a time in our lives when we stare at our current position and ask "how did I get here? Surely this isn't all there is to life." We hide our "pipe dreams" out of fear of failure or ridicule, and God is asking us to give Him those dreams and those desires so He can meet us in those moments of surrender and show us His goodness. In *How Much More?*, Molly invites you into not only getting honest with yourself but with God and sharing your dreams and desires with Him. It's not about spiritual entitlement, but an intentional, authentic relationship with Him - one where we learn how much more our Heavenly Father loves us and desires to give us good gifts."

-Taylor Phillips, Speaker and Author of *Training Ground: From Anointing to Appointing*

The world needs more of THIS. We tend to pray to God about our health, friendships, and family... but why don't we pray to God about the God-sized dreams we have in our hearts? Molly's approach to unpacking the truth behind what it looks like to pursue your God-sized dream is exactly what our generation needs to hear. This book is going to INCREASE YOUR FAITH, and equip you with the tools to step into all that God has called you to be.

- CC Calbonero, Podcast Host of That's Joy (@ccalbonero)

contents

introduction 9
CHAPTER 1: before I formed you 19
CHAPTER 2: a little less filtered 25
CHAPTER 3: a place to dwell 33
CHAPTER 4: bring me a new bowl 41
CHAPTER 5: he will not be delayed 47
CHAPTER 6: it might be unexpected 55
CHAPTER 7: follow my voice 63
CHAPTER 8: a listening conversation 75
CHAPTER 9: keep dreaming bigger 85
CHAPTER 10: purpose in the process 93
CHAPTER 11: when you start to move 101
CHAPTER 12: watching from a window 107
CHAPTER 13: his promise is his presence 113
CHAPTER 14: prepare your table 123
CHAPTER 15: my miracle is your miracle 131
CHAPTER 16: met by authority 137
CHAPTER 17: limitations met by transformation 149
CHAPTER 18: right now on earth 155
CHAPTER 19: with a heart for harvesting 161
CHAPTER 20: directed to your purpose 169
CHAPTER 21: calling him Lord 175
CHAPTER 22: who is able 183
CHAPTER 23: false summits 189
CHAPTER 24: I'm ready 195
notes 203
acknowledgements 205
about the author 209

introduction

Have you ever looked at your life and thought to yourself, there has to be more?

I'm an optimist, almost to a fault. I am the first one to call out a silver lining, and I insist that dire circumstances will get better even if there isn't a glimmer of hope in sight.

I graduated from a great college, earned my degree, and immediately got married. I went on my honeymoon, moved across the country with my new husband, and began an exciting new job.

From the outside, it looked like I had everything I ever wanted. I was supposed to be on this exciting new adventure, but instead, I just felt lost. All of my optimism was quickly forgotten in the life I found myself in; that season is known as "post-grad." Somehow, I felt like my life lacked purpose and fulfillment. I thought I had everything I could ever want. I felt I should be more grateful, and yet, I felt far from God and far from my identity as His. Even though my life appeared good on the outside, there was still this unsettling longing deep in my soul.

how much more?

I couldn't help but think God had to have more for me than this.

If there were a manual for fulfillment, I felt like I had faithfully followed it and taken the steps to find happiness and success. I had an incredible Instagram feed full of mountain views, but in reality, I felt like I was stumbling through a dark valley by myself.

I felt confused. I felt as if I'd somehow woken up one day and found myself inside a life that wasn't meant for me to live. Do you know that feeling?

I had what I thought I should have wanted, but somehow, it still didn't feel like enough.

I didn't know where I was headed or what I wanted, but I knew I needed to make a change.

My husband and I spent night after night discussing how disillusioned we were and how we felt we had done the "right" things, but we still landed in this lonely little mountain town.

We didn't want to keep pushing through because we weren't even sure what we were working towards anymore. I kept thinking to myself this isn't what I wanted because I felt let down and disappointed in what I thought I was promised.

What was I promised?

We had moved to Colorado in faithful obedience, in a moment of passionate risk, while taking lead from the Holy Spirit. I

introduction

thought we would drive up the mountain with angels singing alongside our old SUV. After a year in the mountains, we sat lonely, afraid, and disappointed in life and in God.

I felt like God led us to this lonely mountain town to drain our savings account, to have us spend too many hours in our offices, and to have us live a life without community (I'm an extrovert, so community is a big deal to me).

My husband and I were new to marriage, new to life post-grad, new to our jobs, and new to life out West. I continually questioned if there was more to life than the disappointment I felt.

After a year in Colorado, we were filled with tears and frustration. Both of us were looking at each other and asking the same question: "Where are you, God?" and both of us were taking turns reminding one another He was real even though He felt so far away.

While we wrestled with our desire to move and leave Colorado, we went to visit a bigger church, in a city that was a day trip away. The pastor of this church had spoken at our college chapel, and, after the service, he recognized us and spent time chatting with us about our life in the mountains.

I'm not sure if he could tell by the tone of our voices or if the Spirit prompted him, but he knew immediately we didn't want to be there anymore.

"What do you guys want?" he asked us.

how much more?

That question shocked us. We just kind of stared at each other.

His young son approached us mid-conversation and asked if he could play a game on his dad's phone. The son asked his father, "Dad, what game should I play?"

The pastor replied, "Whatever one you want."

Then, he turned back to us and used that exact moment as an illustration. "God has already told you to play the game. He's giving you the phone, and He trusts you to play the game. Don't worry so much about asking Him where to go or what game to play, just go play," he explained.

That conversation shifted my ideas regarding what God wanted for me and what I wanted for myself. The problem wasn't what I wanted or didn't want, necessarily. It was really just me asking myself if God cared about what I wanted. I think a part of me was afraid to want more because I was afraid God didn't want more for me. I wrote an entire book to tell you He wants more for you than you think.

To discover what God wants for you, you have to trust Him with your desires first. I tried to ignore what I wanted. I was busy pretending I wanted all the things I thought I should want, and I never actually had an honest conversation with my Father about it.

But when I finally did, this was the bravest and most transformational thing I did.

We all want something. Maybe you want to be a leader and

introduction

speak at events, but you've never even led a small group. Maybe you want a crazy dream job like me, desiring to write books, but you don't know how to get there. Maybe you want a house full of kids with your "born to be a dad" type of husband, but you've never dated anyone. Maybe your desire for these things, like mine, takes hold of your mind and lets it spin into daydreams longer than a six-season Netflix show.

We have to start with recognizing we are human, and naturally, we want things.

Then, we have to realize we have a God who actually cares about what we want. When our desires are met with the supernatural power of God, that's when we feel fulfilled and content, and there will be a real kingdom impact for God's glory.

But first, what do you want?

At times, in order to figure out what you want, you have to figure out what you don't want first. At times, I felt wrong for saying I didn't want my present circumstance. It felt as if that wasn't a good enough reason to make changes or decisions. At times, it felt selfish.

Was what I wanted in line with what God wanted for me?

I let my unmet expectations drive me toward asking for more and eventually taking action and allowing God to transform.

I had been avoiding asking myself and God what I really wanted and what He wanted for me because I was afraid. I was afraid He didn't care about what I wanted, and I was afraid that what I wanted was unattainable. What if He couldn't make it happen?

But God is good, and He cares deeply about what we want, even if we don't always receive it.

What if it doesn't scare us anymore if we fall at His feet fully surrendered because what we want is actually small in God's eyes? What if He really isn't limited by us and our dreams and desires are actually an invitation into our destiny?

Maybe, just maybe, looking at what you want and dream about is where the Spirit of God will pull you into a deeper and more intimate relationship with Him than you could have imagined. Maybe facing your unmet expectations or promises from God that are not yet fulfilled will lead you to a place where God can meet you.

I had forgotten that when Jesus saw a blind man on the side of the road, He asked, "What do you want me to do for you?" (Mark 10:51 NIV).

If I had been that blind man, I'm not sure I would have been brave enough to answer.

For a long time, I didn't think I knew the answer myself. Writer and philosopher Dallas Willard famously wrote, "Understanding is the basis of care. What you would take care of, you must first understand, whether it be a petunia or a nation." Before you can care about your hopes, dreams, or desires, you have to know what they are and understand them.

introduction

We need to ask ourselves what we want before we are able to go to God with those things or have an answer when He turns to us asking, "What do you want?"

I didn't really know what I wanted or why. I had consumed too many social media feeds that led me to believe happiness came in the form of a perfect, sustainable wardrobe, an all-white, on-trend kitchen, or expertly captured family photos.

God can't lead us to contentment, true joy, or fulfillment if we aren't able to answer Him when He asks us about what we want.

I knew my life wasn't full of joy or contentment; instead, I felt faced with confusion, unmet expectations, and unfulfilled promises. I had no choice but to start sorting through them. I needed to understand what I wanted before I could care for those dreams. I realized I had to care for them because God Himself might have placed them within me, entrusted them to me.

When I start to clean my closet, the chaos is neatly tucked away behind a closed door where no one can see. But slowly, I have to pull out boxes and clothes, forgotten shoes, and suitcases.

The room becomes cluttered and chaotic as it is full of the explosion that was previously hidden behind a door. As I make decisions about things I throw out of the closet, thinking, I'll deal with that later, there is organized chaos consuming the room. Then, things start to go back into the closet with a new sense of order.

how much more?

It feels so satisfying to close the closet door again, knowing it's a little less cluttered than it was before. But the room had to become chaotic and get worse before it got better. The process of closet cleaning usually means making a mess before you can clean one.

Going to God with my hopes, dreams, desires, and expectations for life felt like this.

I don't know at what point you thought you would "make it" or find contentment. Once you got there, like me, maybe you still felt a longing for more. Maybe you just want more, or you want something else, or you want what is next.

We have to sort through those longings we feel deep in our souls and discover where they come from and where they might lead us.

Just like closet cleaning, occasionally, we have to admit the cute dress from high school doesn't fit anymore, and it's kind of unrealistic to think it might someday. Sometimes, we dig up our old dirty hiking boots and decide to take them for another spin as we revisit a dream we used to have. Maybe it's a combination of both.

An awareness of our expectations can lead us into a life of surrendering them to God, who already knows every desire, longing, and dream we have. Don't forget: He wants to hear about them from us. He is constantly asking us, "What do you want?" My hope for you is that you both understand and care about your answer.

introduction

CHAPTER 1

before I formed you...

I like to be rewarded. If you're like me, you, too, might also have a personality driven by rewards. Maybe you treat yourself with your favorite coffee for meeting a deadline or celebrate with a dinner including friends after getting through a day you were dreading.

It's not a bad thing to want our work to be rewarded. But, it can become unhealthy when we start hoping God will reward us for being good. This makes our relationship with Him more transactional, and ultimately, it lets us believe we have more control than we actually do.

In this mindset, I might expect His graciousness in giving good things to His children to be dependent on their behavior rather than on His goodness alone.

This sense of spiritual entitlement had crept into my life.

I prayed, I read my Bible, and I was so faithful. And yet, I spent days wondering why God wasn't dropping blessings on me because I was so good. Didn't I deserve more? Why wasn't God giving me what I had earned and what I had deserved? I longed for more but felt like I couldn't find the formula to receive it.

Of course, I didn't explicitly say it like that in my mind. But my mindset had been slowly shifting, and it led to great disappointment when the expectations I had were not met. Disappointment is often rooted in misplaced hopes.

My hopes had subtly shifted to being rooted in the outcome of the expectation I had built for myself rather than on what God had planned for me.

I was waiting for my reward for doing the difficult things like loving those who are hard to love, giving generously, or consistently going to church when I really didn't feel like it.

I wanted to feel like my hard work was being seen. I wanted to feel like it was worth it.

Have you ever been invited somewhere and felt like you didn't deserve to be there? I have somehow ended up in a few incredible places where I'm left with my head spinning, thinking, *How did I end up here? Because I clearly don't deserve this.* Maybe it was an opportunity you received or an invitation to be a part of something special.

In one of these circumstances for me, I was the youngest person given an opportunity to be a part of something. I felt they must have made a mistake because everyone else in the room was older, wiser, and more experienced than I was.

I didn't understand why they wanted to give me the opportunity. I wasn't qualified, ready, or prepared. I was incredibly aware of the fact I'd had nothing to do with receiving it. I hadn't done anything to earn this. I just happened to know someone who knew someone, so I ended up there.

I think God is constantly inviting us to places where we might feel like this. He has more in store for us than we can imagine. He gives us favor because of the relationship. He knows us, He loves us, and as our Father, He wants to take us to greater places and allow us to delight in greater things.

He already knows what we are capable of. When we are thinking we are the ones who don't deserve the opportunity, He's already planned an incredible future full of more than we ever could have asked for, and He wants to reveal it to us. It isn't dependent on our ability at that moment. It's simply because He knows us and He sees something in us.

It reminds me of when God called Jeremiah. He said, "Before I formed you in the womb I knew you, before you were born I set you apart; I appointed you as a prophet to the nations" (Jeremiah 1:5, NIV). Like Jeremiah, God has a plan and purpose for your life. Jeremiah's response was one rooted in worry about his lack of ability and experience. But God vowed He would be with Him, and He would equip Him. I think the same is true for us.

Our dreams have everything to do with the God who dreamed them up, along with you, and will walk with you toward them. And when you walk with Him towards your dreams, you'll experience more of Him and of His love.

God loves faithful obedience in our lives. He often rewards us

how much more?

because He loves us. But it isn't about the reward. The outcome isn't in our control. It isn't dependent on the work we do.

It's about the work He already did.

We need to get back to the simplicity of the gospel message. We need to remind ourselves of when we first met Jesus and of that humble feeling of knowing you are receiving something so beautiful and so wonderful, and it is so much more than what you deserve.

We have to understand we are all undeserving of His love, and yet, He is constantly inviting us into a deeper relationship with Him.

When my thoughts slip back into the idea I am doing something for God and am expecting Him to reward me, I have to let the gospel hit me all over again. I have to remind myself God had already given me His Son, the greatest sacrifice He could ever possibly make. You need to start with humility and gratitude as you pursue your hopes and dreams with God.

He gave me eternal life. He sent His Spirit to come and dwell in me so I can live a full and abundant life, impacting the world for the sake of His Kingdom.

I am the one who owes Him something—a life fully surrendered. When the joy of the gospel permeated my life and my thoughts, the disappointment of unmet expectations started to fade away. The focus shifted away from what I thought I deserved (which again, was really nothing) to how undeserving I was and how gracious God was. Thanksgiving and gratitude then took over

before I formed you...

my mind rather than entitlement and disappointment.

And do you know what the craziest thing about God is?

He is a God of more than enough, a God of abundance and generosity. He just wants to be with us, and in return, He will graciously give us all things. It's actually written in His Word. To Him, it's about the relationship.

> *He who did not spare his own son, but gave him up*
> *for us all—how will he not also, along with him,*
> *graciously give us all things?*
> Romans 8:32, NIV

He has been a generous God from the very beginning when He created the world with intricacies and beauty for us to enjoy.

As we explore the dreams and desires we have and how they can be met and fulfilled by God, either in receiving the desire itself or finding fulfillment in the person of God, we have to remember His generosity. He has already given us more than we need and more than we deserve, and He continues to do so.

You don't have to work toward a reward because you never deserved or earned anything you've received from God. He has just been generous and loving in His giving to you from the very beginning.

When I read through the miracles Jesus performed while He was on earth, I see the character of our God as a God of abundance. He takes a loaf of bread and feeds thousands, and He still has food leftover. He is a God who both provides and satisfies.

He knows we get hungry. He knows we have desires, longings, and ambitions. He is able to satisfy our souls with more than enough every single time. He is ready and able to give us all that we ask for and more. But it starts with contentment in just being His.

CHAPTER 2

a little less filtered

Growing up, I was the kind of kid who could never narrow down my list of invitees on my birthday party list. I had an easy time making friends, and I wanted to include everyone. As I grew up, I realized it was easy to make a lot of friends to invite to a party but difficult to find the kind of friends who you could call in the middle of the night.

Building genuine friendships with other people is difficult and maintaining them is difficult too. It takes time, work, and even some conflict. To have genuine relationships with others, one must begin with a genuine relationship with God, knowing Him as a trusted friend.

When girls were mean when I was a kid, my mom would often use the phrase, "They're just jealous," and she was almost always right. She had been around her fair share of mean girls by that time in her life. She would repeat that phrase and assure me no matter how old I got, jealousy would still sneak its way into friendships. She would compare my drama on the middle school bus to the same conversations she was having with women her age.

As an optimist, I wanted to believe it would change and that

how much more?

one day, I would find treasured friendships without the drama. I called my mom confused and upset when, as an adult, one of my best friends started to be incredibly mean to me. I was hurt and upset when my mom responded with her usual, "She's just jealous."

It took me months to realize my mom was right. She *was* jealous, and it was ugly and hard, and it ended in the worst friendship breakup I had ever had. I thought it should have been different because we were "grown-ups" and because we were followers of Jesus.

I wrestled with that friendship ending because I saw all the #communityovercompetition stuff on Instagram, but it wasn't working. It didn't save me from losing a best friend. I was questioning where God was in my friendships and in my community.

I think we spend a lot of time telling ourselves and each other we need to cheer each other on and not be jealous. I've come to realize it's so much more than that. God has more for us in our friendships.

I don't want friendships that simply don't have jealousy present (or any area that hinders your friendships the most). I actually want the Spirit of God to enter in and completely replace that jealousy or sinful nature with something else. I want God to do more in my friendships and in my community.

We have to actively pursue a life without jealousy, and we have to actively choose to put on the Spirit of God instead. This can feel like a continuous battle in our minds throughout the day, especially with all of the curated feeds that are placed before us and ready to deceive us. I had expectations for my community that were not met. I was heartbroken.

I replayed the way I had watched myself invest so much into these friendships; friendships that would end as our lives changed, as we drifted away from one another, or as a messy and disastrous miscommunication built itself up and completely separated us.

I couldn't help but question God's vision and promise for my community.

When I watched the friends I thought I would keep for life disappear as if we'd never known each other, I looked to God with confusion and disappointment. And then, I started to look to Him as a friend.

I found myself feeling a pang of hurt when I didn't have anyone to call, no trusted friend who knew and understood me. Then, the Holy Spirit would remind me He was right there, comforting, communing, and consoling, ready and equipped to be my very best friend.

I hesitantly let go of past friendships that were no longer a part of my current season, and I watched God begin to fulfill my longing for a friend with Himself. I allowed God to do the difficult work of pruning me, cutting away things (and sometimes people) that were no longer a part of His greater plan and purpose for me.

Then, I started to pray for the friends I thought I needed.

how much more?

I waited, hopeful God would drop a few new besties from the sky. I was hoping they would all live near us in Tennessee, all be married like me, have similar interests, have a puppy so we could walk our dogs together, and be on the same timeline as my husband and me for the future.

I imagined all of us living together in our houses with our white picket fences, in the same neighborhood, and growing old together. Maybe some of our kids would end up marrying each other! I kind of have a big imagination. I thought it would be easy to find people who looked like us, thought like us, and who were just like us in every way.

That didn't happen.

Instead, my husband and I spent months searching for a church. We found one, and we started going consistently and praying for friends, but we met very few people in our first year there. We were encouraged to go through a membership class and began volunteering. We were told testimonies about how these were the avenues where God would provide your "people" and your very best friends.

I showed up looking for them. We lingered at every church event, constantly scanning the room, and I volunteered beyond what I had capacity for, in hopeful anticipation of my future bestie walking in the door one day with a golden halo over her head and angels singing beside her. Spoiler alert: It never happened.

Instead, we made a few connections in a few unexpected places. They didn't look anything like my expectations, and at first, that left me confused and frustrated. I wanted the friendship to be easy—I wanted it to feel comfortable. The reality is, that takes a really, really long time, and honestly, the closest and deepest friendships often come out of a little bit of struggle and both people saying, "We are still committed to this."

When I go to God with my array of emotions and my mess of mistakes, confusion, and questions, He doesn't turn away from me. Instead, He brings me closer.

That's the example our friendships should follow, too. I don't think we need friendships that are perfect and seem to match up in aesthetics as our Instagram feeds. We need to pursue each other despite the mess, the heartbreak, and the inevitable hurt. We need to walk through the conflicts courageously when they come, knowing God's heart is for unity, and ultimately, it will only bring us closer.

God didn't put the people who I wanted in my life. He put the people I *needed*. People who challenged me and frustrated me but also people who I could show the love of God to by saying, "I see you, I know you, and I am choosing to love you anyway."

I don't think God intends for our friendships to end in hard, messy ways, and I don't think He intends for us to get hurt in the process. I do know that His plan is to redeem everything, and He provides for us in human friendships, and, in the friendship, we can find in Him.

When I look back on the messy, hard friendship breakup I walked through, the thing that was missing the most was

how much more?

honesty.

We were both frustrated and hurt, but neither of us was willing to do the work of muddling through it and persevering until we made it on the other side. We didn't show up with the hard stuff, and we didn't show up authentically.

As I began to meet new friends, I noticed a lot of women were longing for a deeper community, but not a lot of people were eagerly making the sacrifice to be the first one to open up and be vulnerable.

We all wanted to have comfortable, deep friendships, but we were trying to start by showing up as the best, most filtered versions of ourselves—trying to show each other why we would make a great friend as if we were writing verbal friendship cover letters.

We all wanted to share the most interesting, awesome things about ourselves, but no one was eager to be the first one to say, "Reading the Bible is actually really hard for me," or, "Making friends feels intimidating," or, "I'm afraid this won't ever get better, and I don't see God in it right now."

We have to show up and be honest. We have to be honest with each other about who we are and invite others to be fully themselves with us. The only thing that could have saved my friendship breakup was honesty.

We needed to show up, and do so honestly, so that together we could walk through it, no matter how many awkward conversations it took. When we didn't, we prevented God from healing the wounds we were too busy trying to keep secret.

I think those secret wounds are rooted in competition.

We want to show off the vacation we took to Hawaii on Instagram without putting on display that we stayed at our aunt's house for free and otherwise couldn't afford it. We want to put the fun, exciting things front and center while hiding what really hurts from each other.

We want to hold the hard things close so no one can see them and put all of the good and happy things on display to curate an image of our life that's far from authentic. When we all think that everyone else's curated lives are real, we start to hide what's actually happening in ours.

What's really crazy is being in a healthy, godly community is actually the solution to the problem. If we are open and genuine in our friendships, our hurt will often find healing in and through our communities.

When we aren't honest, we become more competitive, wanting to make sure no one catches us being insecure, unhappy, or walking through a difficult time. We become more isolated and start to believe that we are the only ones.

To stop the cycle, we all have to step out and be a little more honest. We have to be a little more open, a little more vulnerable, and a little less filtered. Every time we are honest, even when it's hard, it invites the next person to say "same," and that's where community starts to really exist and become more meaningful than a hashtag.

how much more?

I want genuine community. I want it so, so badly.

To move into it, I have to admit I really want it, talk to God about it, and do something about it. I can't sit back and expect the community around me to change if I'm not willing to be the person who shows up authentically first.

CHAPTER 3

a place to dwell

My vision of the future involved one place. I had grown up in a family that didn't move around—my mom had grown up in a more tumultuous home, so she was insistent on building us a home and a life that felt more steady. She wanted us to have a home base—a place that was ours.

I always had the idea in my head that wherever I landed in the future would become home, in the kind of way that all of the neighbors were on a first-name basis, and we'd have block parties and deep community with one another.

Even though my older sister had been out of the house living on her own for years, her childhood room still looked and felt like she could walk back in at any time, whether she was twenty-five or twelve. My mom wanted to make sure she knew she had a place that was hers—a place where she would always belong.

Of my sisters, I was always the most independent and the most adventurous. I started my adventure of finding new places to call home for myself when I moved to Ireland for a study abroad program in college.

I had a difficult experience studying abroad, including a tough roommate situation, lots of broken promises, and a lonely semester with only a handful of American students my age on my side of the country.

Despite this, leaving Ireland brought on a mixture of emotions, ranging from sadness to happiness. I spent a semester making a home in Ireland while simultaneously missing the home I left behind in order to study abroad. Returning to the blinding sun in the summer, compared to the gloomy days in which I had spent the last semester, made me feel comforted and known.

While abroad, I was in a missionary program, and some of my classes focused on the life of a missionary. The assigned reading was my favorite part.

The books often talked about home, a concept that was now resonating deeply with my heart as I longed for one home and simultaneously made another. A part of me was missing my friends and family back home, while my present focus was building relationships in my study abroad program. I cared deeply about the people I spent the majority of my time with while I was abroad while living in the tension of knowing it was only for a season. I was learning to navigate this time where I invested in a place I would eventually leave.

This feeling is often the feeling of how we, as God's sons and daughters, are longing to be fully at home with Him in eternity while simultaneously making a home and fulfilling our callings on Earth.

My expectations for one home were beginning to get shaken as I watched God call me to more than one physical space at the same time. I was called to be a daughter and sister in the Chicago suburbs, a student and leader on campus in Indiana, and now, a prayer warrior for the family and home I had made in Ireland.

When my husband and I got married, in our newlywed bliss, we left home with starry eyes and hopeful visions of our future. Within the first few weeks, we started to envision our life in the high Rockies and what a lifetime of dwelling there would look like for us.

We would imagine where we would buy a house, where our future kids would go to school, how our church would grow and change, and how I would someday lead a ministry, even though our current church met in a small corner room of the local library.

I love the high Rockies. Though I had some of my darkest, most difficult moments tucked in the shadows of those mountains, I love them with everything in me. I feel like I can still hear a moose crunching through the snow in our backyard, and I miss the way tourists would ask if we really lived there "like year-round?" Going to the post office reminds me of our home in Colorado because we couldn't get mail delivered to our address in the mountains.

I thought our first big move would be our moment of beginning our life together in our community. I somehow let myself believe and stumbled into the idea that God had promised us a physical dwelling place in this world that would stay constant. Instead, He came to dwell in us (John 6:56, 2 Corinthians 6:16, Revelation 21:3 NIV).

how much more?

I'm not saying it is wrong to stay in the same place your entire life. I do think it is wrong if we do it for our own self-serving comfort, knowing this isn't God's call for our lives. We have to want God's way more than our own comfort, always. We have to be willing to move, in a physical and spiritual sense, when God calls us to. Because He dwells in us, He will go with us.

God often calls His people into motion. It may not mean moving across the country for all of us, but for some of us, it means rearranging our vision and expectations of finding a dwelling place. We need to allow God to give us His vision for our homes with the confidence His way is always better than ours.

I've been rearranging my vision of home as God has allowed us to start to build it, and to be honest, it has been difficult. I've hurt people's feelings, I've lost friends, I've had to say hard goodbyes and uncomfortable hellos. But I've learned that, ultimately, the true, constant dwelling place God gives us is Himself.

The longing I had for a home was met with "this isn't your home; you weren't created for this." When I was longing for a place to belong and feel known, I was told again and again, and, in the best-intentioned way, that I was not made for this world, but instead, I should be looking toward Heaven. That meant the only home that would satisfy me was waiting for me in eternity.

It reduces what God intended for a dwelling place when we start to talk about Heaven in cliches and long for the beautiful and certain future we have in Heaven with our Creator. He came to dwell in you and to be present with you right now. If you're in a difficult season, it might be encouraging to look forward to Heaven. But when I was reminded "this isn't your home" in Colorado, I felt like my ache for a sense of belonging was being dismissed.

I was bothered by that answer. I knew my expectations to have one home, to have a place where I felt known and settled in, like cozying up in my favorite reading chair, weren't always realistic.

I was starting to learn God was a God of motion as He began to call us to move to another unknown place. I was still wrestling with the thought that I wasn't made to be here. If I was made for eternity, and I wasn't made to be here, then why did God put me here?

It seems like a pretty basic question, but for me, the responses I had received weren't cutting it. I knew my heart longed for a home, and I knew that desire was created by God. To me, it seemed like God wouldn't be good if He didn't want to give us a home right now. Not just a physical home, but a place to belong, a place to dwell, a place where we could kick our feet up, wear sweatpants, and be fully ourselves.

Saying "this isn't our home" is true in part, and if that helps motivate you to keep building and working as a follower of Jesus, then go ahead and keep saying it to yourself. If not, let me share what I've learned about a home and a dwelling place.

He made us desire a home, a dwelling place, that can only be found in Him. Heaven is when we can dwell in the fullness

how much more?

of His presence. It's true that we don't get that glorious full presence of God without the presence of sin or evil in the world until we are in Heaven. We also have access to His presence and His Spirit, right here, right now.

God often flips the script, and this is the case with finding homes. Instead of sending us out searching for homes, He comes in and makes *us* His dwelling place when we invite Him in.

He comes to dwell in us.

The sense of belonging we all seek is found in dwelling in God and in Him dwelling in us. God also set up the church for us today, and He dwells in it. The church is His plan for the gospel to advance on Earth, and it's happening now.

So, yes, we are made for the eternal dwelling place we have in Heaven, with the fullness of God's presence, but we are also made to participate in what is happening in the world today.

He came to dwell in us, He allows us to dwell in Him, and He has poured out His Spirit on the church, so we have a dwelling place now. We can feel a sense of belonging and a sense of home wherever we are in the world.

We don't have to wait until heaven for that. Our expectations shouldn't be for a perfect, ideal home, but we can be expectant of God to go anywhere we go in the world and to let us find peace in dwelling. Because He is a good God, and He wants us to feel at home right now.

a place to dwell

My parents reached the stage where it was time to sell my childhood home. Over the summer, I returned, and I did what I thought would be the boring and tedious task of cleaning out the dusty boxes in my childhood closet. Instead, it was a day filled with laughter, tears, and memories.

I found journals filled with my childhood dreams. I'd consistently written again and again, "I want to be a writer." I found old photos of my sisters and me in our Fourth of July outfits on the front lawn with our beagle, who is now long gone. My room became littered with memories, and God was speaking to me the entire day.

Coming home and cleaning out my childhood closet reminded me of who I was as a kid and who God had created me to be all along. It pointed me back to the calling God had placed on my life from the beginning. He'd left a trail on preschool report cards, graded middle school papers, and dreams for the future documented in my childhood journals.

I started to ramble to my mom about what I was relearning about myself, as I went through my closet, and I remembered how she had always left our rooms arranged so that we could come back to them.

As I watched my older sister grow, I thought it was all strange. She went to college, got a degree, got her own apartment in downtown Chicago, and got a fancy job. She was doing good things and accomplishing things, but my mom wanted to make sure that whenever she needed to, she could come back home, see an old stuffed animal on the shelf, and remember.

how much more?

My mom seemed a lot less crazy to me the day I cleaned my room out because I realized what she had done for us is what God is always doing for us. He keeps a room for us in His house. He has a place for us where we can come in, look around, remember who we used to be, and be pointed back to where we should be heading. He lets us come in and take a nap on the bed with our old favorite blanket, to feel safe and to remember.

When we come into His dwelling place, He reminds us who we are, who we were, and who we were made to be. And then, we leave with a little more rest, a little more hope for the future, a little more certainty about our identity, and the dwelling place where we found it.

CHAPTER 4

bring me a new bowl

In a society where we are constantly consuming, we need to change the narrative a bit and realize God is actually inviting us to do *more* than consume. We are meant to be a part of creating. In our obedience to participate alongside His Spirit in the church, I think we will see renewal in our communities and, ultimately, in the world.

When we come with a consumer mindset to church, it's often self-focused—an inward approach. *What am I getting from this? How am I being served?*

At times, the disappointment we find in our communities and churches might be rooted in our mindset of wanting to consume church the way we consume so many other things in our lives.

We are constantly consuming information, news, media, and more. Most of us wake up and immediately reach for our phones to start consuming as we scroll. This attitude has crept into the church and has impacted even the most faithful of believers. Sometimes, I believe we think our role is simply to show up, consume what we like and brush off what we don't like, and then we are off to brunch.

how much more?

That is not what it takes to advance the gospel. Instead, we should be personally impacted by the gospel and motivated to see it impact the next person. I want to see passionate followers of Jesus devoted to taking an active part in advancing the Kingdom on Earth, and I want to be involved.

I want the gospel message to saturate our everyday lives, unlike a Facebook post or an Instagram graphic might on Sunday morning.

We aren't meant to be consumers at church. We aren't meant to hear an inspiring message and some fun praise songs, to shake a few hands, and then go back to our little corners of our communities with an individualized mindset. We are meant to be workers in the Kingdom of God, and that means doing Kingdom work. That means taking an active role in the church. We are each uniquely equipped to do our part as a part of the body of Christ (1 Corinthians 12:27). "From him the whole body, joined and held together by every supporting ligament, grows and builds itself up in love, as each part does its work" (Ephesians 4:16, NIV).

In the beginning, God created. When He created us, He created us in His own image (Genesis 1:27). When we participate and when we create, we are a reflection of God. So much more than simple consumption is required of us because of our identity. When we participate, we are reflecting the nature of God. Even if you don't consider yourself an artist, this quote reminds me of our role as participants and creators in the world. Writer Madeleine L'Engle explained, "...an artist is not a consumer, as our commercials urge us to be. An artist is a nourisher and a creator who knows that during the act of creation there is collaboration. We do not create alone."[2]

Creating and participating, whether it's with art or community, draws us closer to God because we walk in our identities as His kids, reflecting Him as we create, and collaborating with His Spirit as we build something that matters.

We look out at our communities, at our churches, at the way that we see people being loved, and at the ways, we feel like people might be slipping through the cracks. Because of my story, I feel uniquely called to welcome the "new girl." I've been her.

I feel a tug on my heart for anyone who feels overlooked, forgotten, or uninvited because I know what that feels like. Even when I have a group to say "hi" to, I want to be the one looking over my shoulder and seeing if someone else is standing alone because I know what it feels like to walk into a room and not know anyone else.

We look to the ways our stories have impacted us and can impact someone else. We look to how God has uniquely and specifically equipped us. We see a need, and we look to see how our gifts, talents, or abilities could meet or even just contribute to that need. And we take God's invitation to us to collaborate in the transformation.

We need to stop showing up, hoping all of the work is already done for us.

As consumers, we might attend a church that doesn't have the young adults ministry we wanted to serve in and decide to

how much more?

move on to a new church because of that. Maybe we think we need to find a church with a more established ministry because that's what we feel called to. But what if God is actually wanting us to be an active part of building that ministry where we are? What if He wants to use us to fulfill a need? What if turning away is turning down an opportunity to reflect God by building, creating, and transforming?

Frequently, God wants to allow us to be an active part of bringing renewal. He is the One who transforms, but He wants to use us to do some of the work. This is the example I think of in the Word:

> *The people of the city said to Elisha, "Look, our lord, this town is well situated, as you can see, but the water is bad and the land is unproductive."*
> *"Bring me a new bowl," he said, "and put salt in it." So they brought it to him. Then he went out to the spring and threw the salt into it, saying, "This is what the Lord says: 'I have healed this water. Never again will it cause death or make the land unproductive.'"*
> *And the water has remained pure to this day, according to the word Elisha had spoken.*
> 2 Kings 2:19-22, NIV

God is the One who healed the water, but there was an entire community of people who were invited to be a part of God doing the healing work. What began this change was actually the discontentment and disappointment of the people.
God wants to use the disappointment and discontentment we have in our communities to direct us to become the people who, by His Spirit, help to bring transformation. The water

was bad and the land was unproductive. People went to Elisha with their unmet expectations in the same way we should go to God.

I love their hearts in this because they start with compliments. They're quick to point out the town is well-situated, but they have an issue with the water being bad and the land being unproductive. The discontent comes from the water because they aren't seeing their land produce anything since the water is bad.

They're frustrated.

And God uses that.

Elisha, as a prophet, heard from God what to do, but he also invited the people who came to him with that disappointment to be an active part in bringing the change that was needed. He told them to bring him a bowl and to put salt in it. They had to go and do that, to take action, in order for the healing to occur.

Elisha also took action by putting the salt in the water. After those actions were accomplished, the water was healed. God healed the water and, with healthy, pure water, they were able to have land that was producing things again.

God can use our desires and longings to point us towards the things in our communities or in our churches that we might need to take an active role in changing or healing. If you long for something you don't see happening, maybe God is inviting you to take part in a story of creation.

how much more?

If you feel discontentment or disappointment, and you're longing for a change and needing pure water to have productive land, ask God to show you what active steps you could take to be a part of the transformation.

If you are longing for a deeper community, maybe God is nudging you to take the first step in creating one.

If you haven't found people who want to get into the Word of God like you want to, maybe you need to consider how you could be a leader in that way.

If you are desperate for your community to have a conversation that isn't happening, one that could bring healing, maybe the Spirit of God is equipping you to be the conversation starter.

Those desires and longings we have that aren't yet met in our community can help point us toward different roles God has uniquely equipped us to fill. We can either respond by staying in the disappointment, continuing to see what is lacking and feeling let down, or we can go and ask our Father to use us to bring the healing and renewal we want to see.

Real change starts when we look at what we want and start to fill those roles as active participants in the transformation. We have to believe God wants to use us and that He can.

He will equip us. He will do the transforming. He will do the healing. We just need to step into what He has for us. And when we do, we're truly walking in our identities.

CHAPTER 5

he will not be delayed

One night, a good friend came over and flopped on my couch, defeated and disappointed. She'd had a terrible day. She felt she had failed and ruined her chances at pursuing her God-given dream. She felt as if she had no chance of chasing after her God-given dream anymore because the path she viewed to get there seemed completely disrupted. Have you ever felt that way before?

I've learned God does some of His best work with His divine disruptions. Sometimes, we take disruption to mean God wants something different or the timing is wrong, but we need to become experts in discernment so we know when to press in and pray even harder. Disruptions in timing and transformation aren't always from God, but He can always work through them.

As my friend and I talked and prayed about her situation, she laid out the desires and plans she had, the hopes and dreams she had for her future, and explained the discontent she was feeling at the moment.

She had big dreams, but she felt stuck. She wasn't where she wanted to be yet. She wanted more. We prayed, and instead of praying for God to change the circumstances, we prayed as if

how much more?

He already had.

I could see the calling God had on her life and the purpose she could fulfill that would bring a great impact for God's glory. So, we prayed as if He had already changed the circumstances, and we prayed that her plans, even though they seemed disrupted at the moment, would happen.

I used to be afraid of praying out loud in front of other people. I was nervous to say the wrong thing, but I was also nervous to ask for the wrong thing. What if what I wanted and asked for wasn't what God wanted for me?

Here's the thing: it's going to sound over-simplified, but what I have learned is God would rather have us go to Him and just ask instead of not spending time in that relational space with Him, assuming He must want something different for us.

Who are we to assume what God wants for us? Unless we see otherwise in the Word of God, we shouldn't assume God's will for our lives won't allow space for what we want.

At first, I was confused as to why my friend was convinced that her dream for this situation would never happen until she told me what was going on in her mind.

If you'd been with me at that moment, in the quiet of the summer night, you might have heard the words she said and thought they didn't sound like the heart of God.

She told me she wasn't certain what we were praying for was God's will for her. Other people weren't certain it was God's

he will not be delayed

will for her, so she had essentially disqualified herself from working toward this dream because of this excuse we call "God's will."

I heard her say this, and I've heard so many other women say it. Honestly, I've said it myself. What if this thing I want isn't what God wants for me? What if I'm praying for something that God doesn't want? What if it's not in His timing?

When you are chasing after a God-given dream for your life, the enemy will try to creep into your thoughts. He might even mask himself as "God's will," when really, he's sneakily trying to take you away from God's will for your life, using distraction and discouragement. If he can convince you the timing isn't right, he can convince you to walk away from the transformation God wants to do in your life.

The setbacks and the disruptions you face when you are going after God's big dreams for your life do not mean that it isn't God's will or it isn't God's timing. Actually, they're probably a sign that you're getting really close. You're a threat to the enemy because you are so close to the heart of God. You are so close to changing the world, he will do anything to knock you back a few steps.

It's a lot easier to recognize this in other people, which is why I bring up my friend. For me, it's easy to see when someone else's dream clearly brings glory to God. I can see that you think it's logical when you're believing lies the enemy has whispered to you. You're convinced that you are already too late; you think you've already failed. But I know this is the enemy's tactic to convince you there is nothing you can do, so

how much more?

you should stop trying.

Timing is already something we are all aware of that limits us as humans; how many times do we say, "If only we had more hours in the day…"

But God isn't limited by time.

We talk about how God's timing is always perfect, and sometimes, to us it feels like we are the bunny running to the tea party in "Alice in Wonderland" proclaiming, "I'm late, I'm late, I'm late," in the same disorganized flurry of distraction. This is what the enemy wants when you are chasing after your God-given dreams.

When we say God's timing is always perfect, at times, we feel we are encouraging one another, when really we are giving God an excuse, in case He needs it.

If you feel like you're too late to pursue a dream God has put on your heart, or if you feel like you've already failed, you won't keep praying for it. You'll give up on the dream and the hope you have when you face disruption or disappointment, and you'll say it wasn't God's will. But God's timing is always perfect. God doesn't need an "out" from us when it comes to prayer.

He invites us to pray expecting an answer, even though we don't know when the answer will come.

Sometimes, it might be true that it isn't God's timing. But often, that's not a full picture of what is going on in the spiritual

he will not be delayed

realm. There is an enemy, and he is doing everything he can to keep us from accomplishing what needs to be accomplished in and through us for the Kingdom of God right now. How clever it is for him to convince us that we're too late and that we should stop praying and give up now!

In the book of Daniel, we catch a glimpse into the spiritual realm and see what is happening as we pray. The angel says, "Do not be afraid, Daniel. Since the first day that you set your mind to gain understanding and to humble yourself before your God, your words were heard, and I have come in response to them. But the prince of the Persian kingdom resisted me twenty-one days. Then Michael, one of the chief princes, came to help me, because I was detained there with the king of Persia" (Daniel 10:12-13, NIV).

It is a good, faithful thing to want and desire things to happen in God's timing. Imagine yourself sitting in my living room right now, a cup of tea in your hands, and a blanket around your shoulders, telling me you feel like it is too late to go after a dream God has put in your heart. If I could see the discouragement and hopelessness in your eyes, I would look right back at you and say, "That's not God."

That is not God.

God is not late. Your words were heard like Daniel's, your prayers were heard, and your dreams are known by Him. I believe He is coming to respond. Your dream, whether it's to be a mom, to get married, to start a business, or to make a total career 180, is not limited by time. Why? Because you have access to a God who isn't limited by time.

how much more?

If you were in my living room, I would take your hand, and we would go to war by going to God in prayer. We would lean in to the battle, believe He's on His way, and start to rebuke those lies the enemy had so craftily made to look like they were godly.

Let's pray God will move today. One of my favorite verses to pray over timing is this: "Therefore say to them, 'This is what the Sovereign Lord says: None of my words will be delayed any longer; whatever I say will be fulfilled, declares the Sovereign Lord'" (Ezekiel 12:28, NIV).

What if we pray for something God doesn't want or at the wrong timing?

Prayers are powerful, but we can't give ourselves too much credit here. God is always gracious, always kind, and always able and willing to redirect us. He's not going to be upset by us going to Him and asking for desires we have; especially when we go with a heart of surrender that says, *Lord I love you and I want your way, but I also want to give you these desires of my heart and trust you with them.* We are meant to "let our requests be made known to God" (Philippians 4:6, NKJV).

Asking for things is actually a beautiful way to present our hearts to the Father. It shows Him we believe He can actually do something in response.

Jesus' first miracle was turning water into wine at a wedding. Before the miracle, the conversation between Jesus and His mom went like this:

he will not be delayed

When the wine was gone, Jesus' mother said to him,
"They have no more wine."
"Woman, why do you involve me?" Jesus replied.
"My hour has not yet come."
His mother said to the servants, "Do whatever he tells you."
John 2:3-5, NIV

I love what this miracle reveals to us about the character of God. Running out of wine wasn't necessarily an emergency; it wasn't a crazy disaster. It was Jesus deciding to save the hosts at a party from embarrassment. It started with Jesus' mom going to Him and pointing out that everyone wanted and expected wine. She went to Jesus because she knew who He was, and she knew He could do something about it. She believed He would. She knew He was empathetic to the hosts. When He said it wasn't His time yet, she still believed He would do it.

Jesus decided to be compassionate and work this miracle because his mom came to Him and essentially said, "I know who you are, and I know you can do this." She wasn't afraid of Him saying it wasn't the right timing. What I love the most about this is even when He said it wasn't time yet, He did it anyway.

When we ask God, in prayer, to move, we show God we are dependent on Him. We want to rely on Him, and we go to Him because we believe He will come and fill the spaces we cannot fill on our own. It's His choice how He answers our prayers, if He gives us our desires, or if He pours out more of His presence, but either way, we will be better for asking.

When we ask, we should be expectant for God to move, and

how much more?

for God to move soon.

We can pray for God's plans for us to not be delayed, and for Him to move through the distractions and the disruptions that we might not anticipate along the way. He is sovereign in all.

Most of the time, I think it is God's timing. He is eager and ready to move. We get to ask Him in prayer to move in the dreams and hopes we have, and when we do, we show Him we believe He can. I want to see Him show up in miraculous ways in my life and in your life today. He will not be delayed. It's time for transformation.

CHAPTER 6

it might be unexpected

I've been the new girl a couple of times now. In the process of leaving a community behind, picking up in a new place, and looking to build a new community, I've learned quite a few things along the way. If you've ever been new to a place, or new to a community, you've likely had to walk the road of navigating new friendships.

In the process of navigating new friendships, I've had to ask myself about God's vision for friendship and community and address my own. What I found at first felt messy and disappointing because my expectations weren't in line with God.

The underlying truth is still the same: God wants more for you than you think. Even in your friendships, He wants more for you. For God to give you more, you must surrender the expectations and hopes you have for the community first and trade them for His.

When moving to new places or joining new communities, I often long for connection and community. But after a coffee date, I've been ghosted by people who I thought I hit it off with. I have been flat-out rejected by people when I mentioned

how much more?

hanging out, and I've been put off so many times I've stopped trying.

Friendship is hard work.

As the new girl, I would start to look for "my people." There's this concept about having "your people," or "your squad," or "your tribe," and if I'm being honest, I feel like the girl who never had one. I love my friends, but I don't feel like I've ever really had a specific friend group.

At one point in my life, I remember feeling like I finally had one specific friend group to be a part of. Then, when I was chatting with one of the girls in that group, she called it "her friend group." The way she said it implied I wasn't in it. I walked away from that conversation frustrated and feeling left out. Honestly, I think we have all experienced that feeling of being left out before, and we've all probably been a part of creating that feeling even unknowingly.

It's really sweet seeing close-knit friend groups form. They're a gift. We can have those close circles and cherish those long-standing friendships, while also allowing God to do more in our friendships. Often, He wants to stretch us beyond those comfortable, close circles.

I used to look for people who just "get me;" people who had so much in common with me that I didn't even have to work for it, and people who made it a natural, easy thing. Sometimes that happens, but most of the time, it doesn't.

In romantic relationships, we talk about finding "the one." In

it might be unexpected

the church, we've come to understand that there isn't a "one." It's a fun, romantic idea, but ultimately God has given us free will, so we get to choose "the one" who we love and marry, then, God empowers us to stay in love and stay married.

Looking for "the one" is often more harmful than helpful because it can leave us feeling like we are failing, like we are unwanted, like we are incomplete without our other half or maybe not even worthy of love. If you're chasing after the idea of "the one", you'll likely be disappointed when you realize you don't have a perfect match.

That same attitude can happen in friendships when we are looking for that "match made in Heaven" kind of friendship that we often don't get to just stumble into. Friendship takes a lot of hard work, pursuit, and even rejection. My close, comfortable friendships are often hard-fought, and that looks pretty different from this idyllic vision.

I've always had a couple of close friends, but my friendships have often been seasonal. They've grown, changed, and moved alongside different transitions in life.

When I was newly married, I became closer with other married friends, and we grew deeper in those relationships as we navigated together what it meant to be a wife. When we moved across the country again, my friends, who had also been through big transitions, became crucial for me as I adjusted to the new things in my life.

When you are praying for God to equip you with friends and connections, you might find that some of the friends and connections He gives surprise you. The connections God offers us are so much better than we think.

What resulted in disappointment was the idea of thinking I would fall into easy, fast friendships with people who thought and acted just like me and were quick to want to do the same things, think the same things, and respond to life in the same way.

When we look for "our people," we are usually looking for people who act and think like us. At least for me, I know I was looking for people who had all of the things in common with us.

God has more for us than limiting us to just one friend group forever. It's great to have close friends who walk through a lot of your life with you, but we should be open to God stretching us into new relationships or getting us outside of the comfort zones of existing friendships. When we are, our friendships become more rewarding with an even deeper connection, and ultimately, we experience more of God in them.

Friendship can be messy and difficult, which involves interpersonal discomfort, miscommunication, and walking through seasons that require persevering through good and bad. But when we invite God to guide us, it's so rewarding.

God's vision for community includes a diverse mixture of ages, life stages, colors, opinions, and cultures, and God's vision for community means sitting in discomfort with people who act, look, and think differently than us. That's where we learn and grow and experience more of Him.

it might be unexpected

The idea of "our people" means we are looking for people with whom we are comfortable. I think God wants us to get a little bit uncomfortable. Some of my most cherished friends are the ones who challenge me. They call me higher and willingly walk into difficult growth moments. When we have a little bit of discomfort in our friendships, we actually get to walk into even deeper, closer friendships.

The Bible says it like this: "A friend loves at all times, and a brother is born for a time of adversity" (Proverbs 17:17, NIV).

You might have to have an uncomfortable conversation with a friend. Some friends are just for a season. Sometimes, God invites someone into our lives to walk alongside and encourage us in a way that person is uniquely equipped for. God might connect us with someone because being their friend will challenge and encourage us to become better.

At times, God calls us to different places at different times, and occasionally, we have to go in a direction that might circumstantially make a friendship difficult to maintain.

Friendships can be unexpected, difficult, or uncomfortable. You can still have your close circle if you have one, but don't miss out on God's invitation to do more than you expect with new or unexpected relationships in your life.

Jesus spent most of His time with people who seemed like a surprising choice. He spent His time with sinners, with people who were lost, and with people on the outskirts of society—not the kind of people whom a King would spend His time with. This made His leadership stand out and surprise people who saw it. The same should be true of us as His followers.

God has specific people for you. They might surprise you.

It might not look like an ideal, picture-perfect friend group. It might be challenging. It might be unexpected.

We should spend less time looking for "our people" and more time inviting the Holy Spirit to move in our current friendships and to be open to what He wants to do in those friendships.

I want to stop asking God for "my people" and start asking Him for His people.

I want to be open to the Holy Spirit when friendships change and shift, and I don't want to feel let down and lost if friendships feel disappointing or difficult.

If I think His promise means never saying goodbye, disagreeing, or never having hard, uncomfortable conversations that leave me fighting back tears, then I'm going to be disappointed when it happens (because it will happen).

When I ask God to help me find His people, the people He has uniquely equipped me to be a friend to in this season, to use my story, and to love in the way He invites us to, I will never be disappointed. He will provide the people who are needed in each stage of life and each unique assignment.

You will see His goodness as He teaches you to love in ways you never thought you could-as He walks you through hard, difficult conversations, and as His Spirit invites you into

it might be unexpected

conversations you weren't sure you were able to have coupled with love and kindness.

Looking for the people He has for you in your current position puts His love on display to the world, as you love one another in ways that challenge and sanctify you. Asking God for His people allows you to see and know God in the context of friendship as He places relationships in your life that might be unexpected or even unwanted at times.

I want Him to lead you to His people, to empower you through His Spirit to love them, to let your friendships become an act of worship and a reflection of His heart toward His people- to surround you with people who will cheer you on, believe in your God-given dreams with you and push you outside of your comfort zone in the very best way. Even if it doesn't look the way you thought it would, God can do more in your friendships.

Unmet expectations can lead us to disappointment. But rejoicing in the unexpected when it comes, leads us closer to God.

CHAPTER 7

follow my voice

A crucial part of any relationship is communication. Our relationships wouldn't work if we just talked to people and never heard back from them. Consistent communication establishes trust.

Do you have that one friend who you consistently reach out to but you never feel like they initiate communication with you? It can be really hurtful. It feels like you are always the one sending out texts or calls first, and that person could go on without thinking of reaching out to you.

The result is often feeling rejected, not needed, and maybe not even worthy of that friendship. Inconsistent communication can be hurtful, and it can start to erode trust.

I think when it comes to our relationships with other people, we often have a high standard for communication, especially now when we have multiple ways to reach people, and we expect a quick reply.

We expect to hear back from people in a timely manner, and when we don't, it leads to frustration. We are used to being available to other people all of the time through various forms of communication.

This is similar to how we often forget that God is always available to us. In the same way that you're shocked when a friend doesn't react to your message within a few minutes, you should be shocked if you don't feel like God wants to speak into your dreams and hopes for your life.

You should expect to hear from God about what you want and about what He wants for you. In a trusting relationship, there is open communication, and open communication continues to establish trust. To trust in the Lord with all your heart (Proverbs 3:5), you have to communicate with Him.

Maybe you have given up on expecting to hear from God. Maybe you think it's mystical or strange, or maybe you just don't feel like you experience God in that way. It's fine for other people but not for you. Maybe it's possible but not something to expect regularly.

Don't disqualify yourself so fast.

When we disqualify ourselves from something, it is often rooted in unbelief. If you are going to God with your biggest dreams and your deepest longings, you need to believe He actually can hear you, He can speak into them, and He can accomplish them.

To move into open communication with our Father, you have to start with trust.

To have a healthy relationship, communication needs to go

both ways. You need to expect God to communicate with you about what you want. You need to tell Him about what you want, but you also need to allow Him to speak to you about what He wants for you. He will make your path straight when you submit to Him in all your ways (Proverbs 3:6), but to trust Him to do that, you need to know how to listen to His voice.

My husband knows I'm about to get upset if I have to ask him the question, "Are you listening?"

If I have to stop talking and ask him if he's listening because he seems distracted, the message I'm getting from him is what I have to say isn't important enough for him to give me his full attention.

When we share our thoughts, emotions, or dreams with God, we don't have to ask if He is listening. He is always attentive and ready to hear from us. He cares deeply, and He longs to hear about our dreams. He isn't the kind of friend who doesn't text back.

He's even more invested in our dreams than we are because He's the One who gave us them in the first place.

He is not a distant Father who doesn't hear His kids or bother to listen and respond when they ask things of Him. He listens and speaks. God is always eager to speak to us when we give Him the space and time and when we develop awareness to listen for His voice. We should be on the edge of our seats ready for Him to speak and eager to jump into whatever adventure He invites us to be a part of next. When you trust the voice that gives you a new hope or dream, you're eager and available to

how much more?

obey it.

Hearing God's voice takes patience and practice, and sometimes, like Samuel, we are going to get confused.

> *One night Eli, whose eyes were becoming so weak that he could barely see, was lying down in his usual place. The lamp of God had not yet gone out, and Samuel was lying down in the house of the Lord, where the ark of God was. Then the Lord called Samuel. Samuel answered, "Here I am." And he ran to Eli and said, "Here I am; you called me." But Eli said, "I did not call; go back and lie down." So he went and lay down. Again the Lord called, "Samuel!" And Samuel got up and went to Eli and said, "Here I am; you called me." "My son," Eli said, "I did not call; go back and lie down." Now Samuel did not yet know the Lord: The word of the Lord had not yet been revealed to him. A third time the Lord called, "Samuel!" And Samuel got up and went to Eli and said, "Here I am; you called me." Then Eli realized that the Lord was calling the boy. So Eli told Samuel, "Go and lie down, and if he calls you, say, 'Speak, Lord, for your servant is listening.'" So Samuel went and lay down in his place. The Lord came and stood there, calling as at the other times, "Samuel! Samuel!" Then Samuel said, "Speak, for your servant is listening."*
> 1 Samuel 3:2-10, NIV

Samuel was being called by the Lord, but he didn't recognize God's voice. Samuel heard the voice of the Lord but wrongly assumed the voice belonged to Eli. Samuel was familiar with hearing the voice of Eli, so he assumed the voice belonged to

follow my voice

whom he was accustomed to hearing from the most.
Eli was his mentor, and he was obedient to answer Eli's call. This shows us that if we want to hear from God, we first have to become familiar with His voice. We have to recognize who is calling us, and to do that, we have to know what His voice sounds like.

This same idea is found in the new testament, "My sheep listen to my voice; I know them, and they follow me" (John 10:27, NIV). You are willing to take action and be obedient to the voice of God when your relationship with God is rooted in trust. God knows you, and He knows your dreams, and listening to His Spirit leads you to follow Him in faithful obedience.

When I was interning at a ministry, we did a demonstration of this concept. One student left the room and came back in with a blindfold on. She sat in front of a room of students.

While she was out of the room, we were all told to pick an action phrase like, "Sit down," and we were to choose a different phrase to say. When she came back in, we were all told to repeatedly, at the same time, shout the phrase we had picked. Our pastor had chosen her for this demonstration because her best friend was also in the room. She stood closest to her, and while everyone else was instructing her to do other actions, her best friend stood beside her saying, "Follow my voice, follow my voice."

I always remember this demonstration because although a room of people shouted other instructions to her, this student chose to follow the voice of her best friend instead. I am reminded of this truth: we listen to the voice we know the best and trust the most.

If we do the work of meeting God and communing with Him, and if we spend time getting to know Him, He becomes our best friend and the most trusted voice of authority in our lives. Like the Psalmist, we say, "Let me hear in the morning of your steadfast love, for in you I trust. Make me know the way I should go, for to you I lift up my soul" (Psalm 143:8 ESV).

When we trust God as the One with authority, the One who will lead and guide us, it doesn't matter how many other voices are shouting at us and instructing us to go in different directions. We will only focus and fixate on the instructions from one voice. The voice we know the best and trust the most is the voice we will follow.

Samuel heard a voice and assumed it belonged to who he knew and who he was used to following and obeying. He assumed it belonged to the person whom he comfortably looked to for instruction, for guidance, and for clarity. Similarly, we would likely choose to follow the voice of our best friend.

We need to know the voice of God so we can recognize it when He calls us, even if there are other voices and other distractions trying to get us to go in a different direction.

When promises are unfulfilled and expectations are unmet, a lot of people are going to have something to say. Who are you going to listen to? When you really want something, but it seems impossible, who are you going to let speak into that? You need to know God's voice so you recognize it when He calls you.

follow my voice

The best way to become familiar with God's voice is to get to know Him through His Word. His voice is clearly defined throughout scripture.

As we come to understand and know His character, we can recognize His voice more easily when He calls us. We start to build trust with Him in prayer and intimacy, and when He speaks, we'll be ready to be obedient because we know His voice and want to follow the One we trust.

We can be confident His voice belongs to Him because we know it is consistent and unchanging throughout all time, and He will never speak anything that isn't in line with the Word.

When doubt, uncertainty, and fear start to creep in, we have to be able to remind ourselves those things aren't God. The best way I know how to discern God's voice is to be able to measure my thoughts and attitudes against God's Word and to look to scripture to see if what I think I'm hearing from God sounds like God's voice.

One clear example of this type of discernment that has shown up in my life many times is fear.

Jesus leads with peace, God leads with love, but the enemy leads with fear. Of course, there is a healthy fear and reverence of God, but the fear I'm talking about is the fear that makes a shiver run down your spine and sends your head spinning down all of the "worst case scenario" situations.

This showed up in my life when I felt the Spirit of God prompting me towards taking a pretty big risk. When I listened to other voices, they encouraged me to plan ahead, to take a longer time to make the decision, and ultimately, to rely on myself.

But that prompting I felt from the Spirit wouldn't go away. It kept coming back to occupy my thoughts, and I still couldn't quite tell what voice was God's.

What if I made the wrong choice? What if all these other voices were right, and this wasn't a wise choice? What if God didn't provide for me? What if I regretted this decision?

One morning, I quieted my spirit and sat down to read the Word and talk to God about this decision. I wanted His will, I wanted His way, and more than anything, I wanted to be obedient and faithful to do what He had called me to do.

That morning, I started to ask God if He would show me which decision was the best decision. Then, in my spirit, I heard God's gentle, loving voice ask, "What's stopping you from making this decision?" I simply thought *I was afraid.*

I was immediately convicted, realizing I was so afraid of the future that I was stuck. I wasn't trusting that God had a plan for me; instead, I was focused on what I was afraid of and all of the worst-case scenario possibilities I had come up with. My mind was full of doubt and fear, taking up space where Jesus wanted to give me peace and confidence in Him.

The verse that came to mind was, "There is no room in love for fear" (1 John 4:18, MSG).

follow my voice

My mindset immediately shifted because I realized it was God who had been asking and encouraging me to move into this transition season all along. He was waiting for me to trust Him. He was waiting for me to stop letting fear drive my life and to look to love instead.

I looked at all of the thoughts, doubts, and fears I had about the decision, and I started to realize they didn't line up with who God was and what God said. God didn't desire for me to make decisions based on my fear of the future. God promises provision, hope, and love.

My fear of regretting my decision and my fear of the future were keeping me stuck in indecision, and it wasn't from God. God wanted to lead me into a deeper place of trust. He was asking me to take a step of faith and to watch Him move in my life.

It wasn't an easy decision, but once I made it, I was able to look to God to provide for me, and I held onto the word He had given me that day—that He was going to lead me with love, not with fear.

I recognized His voice, and I recognized the voice that wasn't from Him. He didn't want me to let fear and indecision paralyze me, and He didn't want me to be confused. He wanted me to trust Him, so I chose to follow His voice even when other voices were directing me in other ways. I watched as God positioned me for what He had planned for me next.

If you're anything like me, you're probably thinking to yourself that it sort of makes sense that I thought God was speaking to me, but what if I got it wrong? Or, what if I still wasn't sure it was God?

Samuel goes to Eli three times before Eli recognizes Samuel is being called by the Lord. Samuel isn't even the one who eventually realizes the voice of God is what he's hearing. It's Eli.

This reminds me of how important it is to surround ourselves with people who both know God and recognize His voice.

We might miss what God is saying to us. We might be stuck in confusion or too distracted by all the voices that surround us every day. Maybe we aren't able to follow those gentle instructions given by our best friend because all of the shouting from social media feeds and news channels confuse us. We have to look to our Eli and say, "Hey; I think this is God calling me, but I don't know for sure. Do you think it sounds like Him?"

I love when God chooses to confirm something I've been praying for through another person in my life. It encourages me that I have heard His voice, and it also invites someone else to be a part of the testimony. Praying for miracles is so much more fun with good company.

God has done this time and time again in our marriage. My husband and I will both pray separately about something; then, when we come together and talk about it, we both get the same answer. We take that as a confirmation that it was from God. One time, we both asked God for a specific number to give. When we both got the same number, we took out the checkbook and wrote it in.

When God gives you a big, crazy, or maybe even scary dream, it takes a lot of boldness to pursue it. In my experience, the easiest way to walk in obedience towards the dreams God gives you for your future is to have already established a trusting and conversational relationship with Him.

When learning to hear the voice of God, He has to become our best friend, our most trusted source for instruction, and the voice we are most aware of. It's hard work. It takes time and investing in hearing from God and getting to know Him, but having an all-knowing, all-powerful God be your guide throughout life is so worth it.

In seasons of uncertainty or when we want an extra boost of confidence, we can also surround ourselves with people who know His voice. It's important to have people who can affirm what we hear by saying, "Yep; that sounds like God."

The more you go to the Word of God, the more you read and see who God is, and the more you worship Him and speak to your spirit about His character, the more easily you'll be able to hear Him.

To trust God with the things you want, you have to trust that He's capable of delivering but also that He wants to speak into them. He's listening, and He probably has something to say. He knows your dreams, and He knows the steps you need to take to pursue them.

I'm confident when you go to Him with what you want, He's

how much more?

going to respond, not only through His peace and presence. He wants to speak directly to you and into your circumstances. When you go to Him, be prepared to listen too.

CHAPTER 8

a listening conversation

Prayer is something that comes pretty naturally to me. I'm an instinctive communicator. In fact, I'll often over-communicate. I'm the kind of person who sends texts that are a paragraph long, I'll write for hours on end, I fill journals quickly, and if you call me, it'll be at least an hour-long conversation every time.

I love to talk, and I love to listen—I love being heard and making sure other people feel heard. For me, the easiest way to think through something is by thinking out loud and communicating with someone else. Revelation often comes the moment I start to say something out loud to someone else.

The same joy I find in communicating in my everyday life has carried into my prayer life.

Prayer can be difficult. My expectations for prayer have shifted the way I've viewed it, and at times, my expectations for prayer have left me feeling disappointed and frustrated with God.

I know God is good—this is the foundation of my faith. Prayer can, at times, complicate that for me. It can feel disappointing when we go to God in prayer and don't receive an answer, or the answer we wanted. It can even cause us to start doubting God's goodness or His involvement in our lives.

The first time I felt really known and seen by God was in a little church in rural Indiana. I was a freshman in college, and the whole "church" thing was still a little confusing to me. At the time, I didn't read my Bible consistently. I had more questions about who God was than words to describe Him. I was starting to think I might need to transfer schools because at my Christian college everyone was talking about a God they knew, and I felt like I was the only one who didn't really know Him.

I believed God existed, and I felt like I had a relationship with Him, but it wasn't personal or intimate at that point. I had imposter syndrome, and I felt like I was pretending to be someone I wasn't by believing in a God who wasn't entirely real to me yet.

At this church, they had a special time of prayer after every service. After watching the long line of people wanting prayer in the center aisle week after week, a classmate of mine explained how profound this experience could be for me and encouraged me to jump in line the next time if I felt God leading me. The next week, a combination of curiosity and the Spirit of God led me to the line where I stood twisting my hands around and trying to look busy and avoid eye contact with anyone watching.

At the front of the prayer line, there were a few strangers ready to pray for me. They explained how they were going to ask God about His original design for my life. Who had God

a listening converstion

created me to be when He originally created the world? They explained how, in Scripture, God created the world with me in mind, and He had a plan and purpose for my life. They wanted to ask Him about it and share that vision with me.

These strangers began to speak God's vision for my life over me and tell me things so specific to who I was and who I wanted to be, that I felt as if they were reading pages out of my journal.

I felt my whole face light up as I suddenly realized the God who created me knew me. He saw me. He cared about the little things, and He was repeating them back to me. He knew the depths of my dreams, goals, and desires. He knew my fears, my hurt, my pain, and He was there, right there, in that little church in Indiana, ready to speak to me.

The following year was a year of pursuing open lines of communication with the Father. I scheduled in time to pray around my college classes. I spoke with God while I walked around campus, and I stayed up with Him into the late hours of the night. I found His Word inviting and energizing, and I would read and read and seek to know Him like I now understood He knew me.

My relationship with Him became conversational, personal, and intimate.

Throughout college, my love for communicating with God grew. It was a passion I would eagerly share with anyone who listened. God speaks! God listens! God cares about what I have to say!

how much more?

My simple prayers would get answered, and I would be amazed and grateful as I shared the little testimonies God was creating and using to build my faith. I would pray for time to study for a test, then a class would get canceled, and I would go tell people in my dorm about how God had answered my prayer.

However, life post-grad was complicated. I was thrown some curveballs I wasn't expecting. I was living in new places, experiencing hardships I'd never navigated before, newly married, and without a strong community around me. I turned to God in prayer.

My prayer life was becoming a little less joy-filled and a little more like a laundry list of things I wanted or thought I needed. I would sit and pray for hours, asking God to move in the situations that made me feel desperate, hopeless, and alone. I felt like I was begging God to just show up in some small way because I felt like I hadn't seen Him in a while.

If He is all-powerful, why doesn't He change these circumstances? If He is loving, then where is my deliverance? If He is kind, why doesn't He want these good things for me that I so eagerly desire? God, where are you?

At times, it felt like the God who knew me and loved me had gone silent. I knew the Word said He heard my prayers, so I felt like I was staring at my own messages with a "read" receipt underneath them, waiting for my friend to reply. I would reread my messages and wonder, "Did I say the wrong thing? Is He mad at me? Does He not care?"

Just like when our friends forget to text us back when we pour

a listening converstion

out our souls over iMessage, it left me feeling forgotten. I felt I was invisible to God, and even worse, if He did see me, I was wondering why He was leaving me alone in the midst of my struggle. Maybe you've felt that way too.

His goodness was suddenly shifting into a big question mark in my mind, and the reason was because of my expectations of prayer.

What do we do with unanswered prayers? If the promise is God hears, and He speaks, why was I so often sitting in my living room thinking neither was true?

I felt like my big dreams were going unnoticed by God, and that hurt.

There are a lot of reasons why prayers go unanswered. I can't list all of them, but I can get into one that changed my disappointed expectations about the things I wanted.

In prayer, I was focused on asking God to move—begging Him to move—I had let my eyes drift towards my disappointment in what I felt like God was or wasn't doing in my life, and I forgot to take a look at the full picture. A lot of us get lost in this logic every so often.

When you want something good, and you believe God can give it to you, but He hasn't yet, don't forget there is more to the spiritual picture.

You might pray and ask God to do something, and when He doesn't answer the prayer, you might assume He doesn't want to do what you asked for. Maybe you'll start to think it wasn't in His will or He doesn't want it for you.

The outcomes of our prayers don't tell us who God is, but sometimes, when our prayers go unanswered, we start to let unanswered prayers shift our view of God.

The Bible warns us that we have to be alert and on guard because the devil is prowling around like a roaring lion (1 Peter 5:8), and he is looking for every opportunity to make sure we are drifting farther and farther from God. The devil wants us to start to doubt whether God cares about what we're asking for when we don't see an answer. Really, he wants to convince us to doubt whether God is truly good.

I started to doubt God's goodness when it seemed He wasn't moving or doing what I was praying for, and all of my prayers were requests. Then, one day, in the shower (If you don't get your best ideas in the shower, we can't be friends), I felt like the Holy Spirit spoke to me and forever changed the way I viewed prayer.

The disappointment I was facing in my life wasn't from God. It was a result of my very human emotions that couldn't be trusted (Proverbs 28:26). I felt like God wasn't listening or didn't care because I wasn't seeing what I had been praying for.

My faith had become dependent on an outcome.

God was wanting me to lift my eyes to the bigger picture. He was busy fighting the battle He had been fighting for me all

a listening converstion

along, but He wanted to invite me to go into war with Him. Jesus came and gave us His authority. I wish I'd remembered to use the authority He gave me more often.

Instead of praying *for* things, I started to ask the Spirit of God what I needed to be praying *against*.

My eyes were opened, and with a new vision, I could see so clearly what was happening.

God wants to answer your prayers *for* friends, but you need to be praying *against* the spirit of division and disunity in the church and some of your relationships.

God wants to answer your prayers *for* provision, but you have to be praying *against* the spirit of delay and distraction, as the enemy tries to get you to walk away from opportunities God is calling you to.

God is prepared to answer your prayers *for* a breakthrough, but you need to be praying *against* the things that the enemy is using to try to prevent it.

Our prayers can become weapons, and you will fall more in love with the God who sees and hears you, as He uses every single prayer.

Prayer is not a transactional conversation like you might be used to. You send an email, and you expect a response. You send a text, and you expect to hear back or at least get a reactive little thumbs up. With God, we often expect Him to move in a time frame that feels appropriate to us, such as five to seven business days. Honestly, we would pay for faster shipping if it was an option.

In prayer, we need to approach it with the mindset and time frame of eternity. It's almost impossible to do this, at least that's how it feels to me, in a world where most things in life come to us immediately or in a time frame that we can control.

Prayer isn't like that, and my expectations for prayer are like putting in a to-go order and then showing up at the next window like, "Ok, God; I'm here. Where's my order?"

Prayer is more than just talking and listening; although, it is both of those things. It is also just hanging out, spending time together, and just being in each other's presence.

Abiding in the Lord is what brings peace, comfort, and joy into my daily life, and He says when you abide in Him and Him in you, that's when you bear fruit (John 15:4).

Sometimes, with my husband, I just want to be near him. I just want to tell him about something that happened to me without him feeling like he has to fix it. For a while, in our marriage, that was really hard for him to understand.

He's a problem solver, so he wanted to be there to solve my problem, whatever it was. However, I usually didn't want him to stand up, walk out the door, and go do something about it. I wanted him to just be there with me in my pain to say, "I understand," and to empathize and allow me to be heard.

When we realized this was a pattern in our marriage, when I

a listening converstion

had a day where I just needed him to be there for me without suggesting solutions to the problem, I'd started by saying, "This is a listening conversation." That became my husband's cue to quietly listen to what I was saying, to learn how I might have been hurting, and to just hold my hand and say, "I'm here. I hear you."

I became disappointed with God when I expected Him to move immediately or in the timeframe that seemed right to me, and He didn't. I assumed this meant He didn't care about what I was praying for.

In prayer, sometimes God wants to spend time with us in what my husband and I would call "a listening conversation." It doesn't mean we won't talk about a solution at all; it just means we aren't going to stand up and go solve the problem right away. First, we are going to spend time together. God is inviting you into "abiding."

There is a lot God can do for us, and He is a good Father who loves us and will take action on our behalf. We should ask Him for our specific desires, needs, and requests.

We should also want to sit in the space in between with Him, to soak in His presence, and to just be with Him and rest in His love.

When I'm in that space, I often leave that time of prayer not thinking of what I had prayed for or wondering when God will show up, but instead, I leave with pure confidence that God alone is enough.

how much more?

I don't wonder if He is going to show up and do what I want. I know He's already doing things for me that I can't see, and I can trust and rely on Him still. Instead of wanting more from my life or my circumstances or a specific outcome, I leave just wanting more of God because His presence is what satisfies.

Being with Him in a pure, intimate moment is what allows me to walk into my circumstances on a given day, whatever they may be, with joy and perseverance because I'm known by, and I know, the One who created me.

When you go to Him with what you want, He might not change everything right away. But I hope you can feel His presence with you, as if He is holding your hand, listening and gently reminding you, "I'm here, I hear you."

CHAPTER 9

keep dreaming bigger

Small Christian colleges are places that feel a little more like summer camp than they do school. Ours had a ton of programming, and there were a couple of hot topics on Christian college campuses that could pop up as a chapel message any number of times without anyone questioning. One of those things was your "calling." We even had a center on campus called the "Calling and Career Office."

Throughout my time on campus, I was quick to ignore the Calling and Career Office and the services it offered. I knew the path to my calling was going to be a messy one and sitting in an office poring over possible summer internship options was not likely going to help.

At that point, I cared more about writing than I did about the calling. I just wanted to write. In my free time between classes, I'd dodge social obligations and occasionally carve out the time to write something that wasn't for a class or a writing assignment but just for me.

My last semester of college was in the fall. By that point, I had gained some crucial relationships with professors who helped me cruise through my final semester while simultaneously

how much more?

planning a wedding and trips with my fiancé to job hunt.

I needed one more credit for a speaking requirement, but the class was full. I emailed the professor asking him if I could please be in his class, and he agreed on one condition: He wanted me to be his assistant and lead class discussions.

I loved this professor and his class. Sitting around and talking was kind of my jam, so it was going to be the perfect credit hour to fill that final spot. This professor picked books, let us read them, and discuss real-life things. I wish I'd known then that we were really just a book club with a great guide. In retrospect, I'd love to go back into that room and ask a few more questions.

One of the classes he taught was on work and rest. The book he chose became one of my favorite books, and the author became someone whose books and podcasts I soaked in religiously.

At the time I read it in college, I didn't have too many deep thoughts about calling, but I did realize there was a relationship between work and rest that God set up for us to enjoy. I scribbled in the margins of the pages about work. I wrote down what I was good at, what I was gifted at, and what I was interested in, and I felt that passionate fire in my belly, knowing the Lord made me for a purpose and with a specific *calling*. I was ready to get out into the world and be used by God.

Then, I graduated college, and I got lost.

Or, maybe I just got distracted. I shuffled out of school with my degree and basically went straight down the aisle to get married

keep dreaming bigger

as soon as I could. We were off to Hawaii for our honeymoon, then cruising with a U-Haul across the country to Colorado.

I started my first big writing project while tucked away in our dark little condo in a ski town. I was passionate about the project, and when my husband came home from his more traditional office job, I would tell him all about what I had learned and researched and written about that day.

But, I was lonely sitting in the condo by myself all day. Our condo was a six-month rental, so it didn't feel like it was ours. There was no office space or desk, so I would often write sitting on the floor with my computer on the coffee table. This wasn't the image of the future I'd had in my mind, so I started to actively try to change it.

As I prepared to graduate, it felt like everyone around me was accepting big, fancy job offers, and once again, I felt overlooked by God. I wasn't sure what I wanted to do after college, and one of my professors continuously told me I was an excellent communicator, and, in some shape or form, I would find a career involving communication. My professor had given me some critical advice, "When a student tells me they got their dream job, I tell them they aren't dreaming big enough. No one should get their dream job right out of college."

He was excited for students who were moving into the workforce to pursue exciting opportunities, but he was also telling us not to limit ourselves to having our "dream job" right away. If you get your dream job right out of college, what does that mean for the rest of your career?

how much more?

I think his advice often reminds me of the heart of God for our hopes and dreams.

At the time, it was encouraging to know I shouldn't be getting my dream job right away. Every day, it felt like I had to see another Instagram post of someone sharing about what they were doing after college and how specific and important their role was.

I told myself during this time, "It's ok that you don't have your dream job yet; keep dreaming bigger," but I didn't realize then how long I would be whispering that encouragement to myself. Even now, my professor's words challenge me to think that God is still inviting us to dream even bigger and want even more for our careers and our lives.

After I wrapped up my first big writing project, I had been furiously looking for a full-time opportunity in the mountains. The image I had in my mind of what I needed to do at the time had nothing to do with what God was calling me to do and everything to do with what I thought other people wanted me to do.

On phone calls, friends and family were always asking, "How's work?" At dinner parties, the first question asked had shifted from, "What's your major?" in college to, "What do you do?" in adulthood. I was grasping at straws to find what I thought other people might think was a good, impressive answer.

In finding an answer to the "what do you do?" question, I lost sight of asking God what He wanted me to do. I was too busy looking at what I thought was an unfulfilled promise. I should

keep dreaming bigger

have been looking at God.

I thought what I was doing was what I was supposed to be doing to walk into the thing we refer to as "our calling," but really, I was just wandering around without asking God for direction in my life.

My expectations for work had been the cute, romantic comedy kind of expectations for work. I wanted to go on fancy lunch dates with my husband, be writing on a big whiteboard on my office walls, casting vision for my next big project, and wearing an outfit that was straight off a trendy business woman mannequin.

We were supposed to be DINK, *double income, no kids*, and with that double income, we should have been traveling the world, going on extravagant date nights, and hosting dinner parties with all of our fancy friends. After all, the first few years of marriage were supposed to be the *best*!

The reality was, we spent it eating out most nights at fast, casual places because both of us came home from long days too exhausted to cook. On the weekends, we spent our time sitting around saying, "Thank goodness it's the weekend," until it was over.

I hated my relationship with work.

I felt like there was nothing in the world I was good at that could also produce a living or give me that feeling of purpose I so deeply desired. I was looking for the calling I thought I should have, instead of looking for the calling God actually

how much more?

had for me.

When I quit my job, I felt like a failure, and I didn't understand what I was supposed to be doing with my life. I didn't know where a sense of purpose came from, and I was disappointed that my career hadn't worked out how I had thought a "calling" would.

My expectations had led me to believe that finding your calling was like panning for gold. I thought I would just keep sifting through all of the options, and sure, there would be the occasional fool's gold, but eventually, I would find true gold. Cue the happy music, and let the credits roll because, at that point, I would have it figured out.

I thought I had to have one calling, and often, I found in conversations, I wasn't the only one. I thought when I found my one calling, my one true purpose, there would suddenly be contentment, joy, and fulfillment. But this philosophy didn't feel freeing to me.

Instead, it felt like I would become enslaved by the idea I could only do one thing, and I wouldn't be happy or content until I found it. This idea also prevented me from realizing that God can call us to different things in different seasons. Leaving one calling behind and entering into a new one wasn't a failure. It was moving with the Spirit of God when He called. And life with God results in Him continually calling us into new, greater, and better things (2 Corinthians 3:18).

My calling reminds me of road trips. My husband grew up in a road trip family, and I did not. My family lived close to the airport, so we would often fly places, and my dad's job provided us with lots of travel deals, so we were not the kind of family who would load up the car and drive somewhere, especially not for fun.

But my husband's family has more of the traditional midwestern vibe—if you can load up the car and get there in under twelve hours, that's just one day's drive, so it's a great idea to do it. It took some adjusting for me to understand how road trips can be fun.

At first, I didn't really understand my husband's relaxed approach. I would just count down the hours until we arrived at our destination. When we drove, he felt like we could take our time to do absolutely anything we might discover along the way because the point of the trip wasn't to get where we were going. In my husband's mind, once we were in the car together, we were on vacation. He had the mindset of endless opportunities and fun to be had.

Driving home from one of our first road trips together, we were packed up, and I had those post-vacation blues. But my husband had a different perspective.

We ended up stumbling upon a national park we hadn't been to, so we parked and took in the views at an overpass, which made the drive home way longer than it needed to be.

Our callings are like that. From time to time, we get hung up on the destination, and we want the faster route. We'd rather hop on a plane and be in one of the first groups to board and among the first to get off when we arrive at the destination.

how much more?

He wants to be with us on the journey though, and the journey and all of the experiences we build along the way in our relationship with Him matter the most. Occasionally, I'm disappointed when I feel like I haven't arrived at the destination fast enough. But I have to remind myself there's a purpose in the process. There are things God needs to show me and teach me on the way.

Here's something funny about the previously mentioned road trip: I remember what we did on the drive home better than I actually remember what the vacation itself was like.

My husband has converted me into a road trip person. Now, when we plan a trip, once we pick a destination, I'm quick to pull up a map and check for anything that might be worth stopping and seeing along the way. There's usually somewhere worth stopping, and it might end up being the most memorable part.

CHAPTER 10

purpose in the process

Have you ever felt like you don't have a purpose? The feeling of purposelessness overcame me while I was looking for a job and trying to find a place for myself in the workplace.

I spent so many nights talking to my husband about how I just didn't feel any purpose. He had a job where he was needed. People had questions for him at work, he had to respond to emails and show up on time, and people would notice if he was gone. He thrived at his role, and it seemed like he was specifically designed for that office. I didn't have that.

He would come home tired but usually excited to tell me about how he'd saved someone money on their taxes and how his financial plan was going to help someone else achieve their lifelong dream of buying a vacation home or paying for their kids' college. He found so much purpose in what he was doing; he was bursting with passion and overflowing with joy.

I didn't recognize that same sense of purpose in myself. It felt foreign to me.

I was in a new place, with a few new friends, searching for a church home, and spending my days sifting through job applications wondering if God had a plan for me. I listened to so many career podcasts, read motivational books, and wondered if God saw me right where I was. Did He care about the dreams I had for my future? They felt so far off and distant, so God started to feel that way too.

If you've ever felt this way, you know what it's like to long for a sense of purpose and belonging. I was looking to find a place for the gifts and talents God had given me, when, all along, He was offering me a sense of belonging in Him.

God made you, and He formed you. He knows your specific gifts and talents intimately. He gave them to you; He's entrusted them to you. But He doesn't leave you on your own to accomplish anything. Actually, we can't accomplish anything without Him.

If you feel like you should be doing more, or if you feel lost and like you don't know what to do next, be patient. God knows our big dreams because He imparted them to us.

At times, it can feel like you're staring at a solid rock wall that needs to be climbed, but you can't find a single place for a foothold to get started. It can make you feel lost and abandoned, and you might even start to wonder what is next for you. What does the future hold?

Maybe you're searching for clarity in a particular area of your life. Maybe it's your career, maybe it's your friendships, or what college to go to, or where to live. Maybe the clarity comes not when we feel like it's all illuminated to us (because it never really will be) but when we choose to be reminded of

purpose in the process

who God is and who He says we are.

Occasionally, we need other people to remind us of who we are. When I start to get a little distracted or a little overwhelmed, the people who know me best are able to lovingly shift my eyes back to what matters most and to help me to focus. When I get confused, they are able to shake me out of making decisions that don't make sense.

Often, seeing what works for other people makes us think it should work for us too. "Comparison is the thief of joy" especially when it takes our eyes away from the unique things God wants to dream up with us. God has so much more for you than trying to fit you into something that might be great for your neighbor but not for you.

For example, I don't like routines. I don't like showing up to the same place every day. I've always thrived in having a diverse schedule that changes constantly, letting my brain jump from one thing to the next. I can't sit and focus on one task uninterrupted for hours—I'm a multiple coffee breaks kind of person.

I used to hate that about myself, but I slowly realized God had created me for something specific, and even the quirks and little details we think are amiss are infused with intention. He doesn't make mistakes. His power is made perfect in our weakness (2 Corinthians 12:9).

He knows the ways you work well, and He knows the ways you mess up. He can use all of those things for His glory.

how much more?

You can rest in knowing God designed you for work that matters both to Him and to you. He has a purpose for you, and together, you can accomplish it with Him. He designed you for it. His Spirit will empower you to push through the things you feel aren't your gifts.

The gift and the calling actually don't matter that much—what really matters is He is an all-powerful God, and you're His kid.

Parents are usually really good at reminding us of who we are because they've watched God form us throughout our whole lives. My parents always knew I would write, and they always believed in my dream, even when I didn't.

When I was searching for a purpose, my parents graciously directed me. One Christmas, my mom gifted me with a membership to a writing program I could do online while I was working my other job. The membership landed in my email box, and not only did it come with a renewed sense of purpose, but it also came with my mom saying, "Hey, focus! This is something I see in you. You were created to do this. I believe in you. Keep doing it."

My husband has done this for me time and time again. He helps remind me my words are worth writing, and to other people, they're worth reading, even when I don't feel that way.

I think God has that same role in our lives. He wants us to look to Him for our identity, and He wants to call out the things He sees in us, even when we don't see them yet. Maybe you don't see yourself as a leader, but God might see that in you. Pay attention to the opportunities that He is gifting you because

purpose in the process

they might give you direction towards a purpose He wants to fulfill in your life.

God has a purpose for every season, and even when it is full of messy, hard things that are unexpected, He can redeem anything and use it for His purpose. Ever so often, our lives don't reflect what God originally designed them to be when He formed us and made us.

We have to pray and ask God to direct us to who we were made to be and to guide us back to the original design He had for the world and for us in it.

In His Word, He constantly reminds us we have a purpose. I thought, when I found the "calling" and the career I was made for and gifted in, I would have purpose.

But there is so much more to it than that.

God is inviting us to have purpose in Him, right now, while we are on the journey. With all the failures, mistakes, and wrong turns, He wants to continuously be on the journey with us, ready to lock eyes with us and say, "Hey. Pay attention. Look at me, and I'm going to remind you who you are."

Purpose is a lot less about what we are doing and a lot more about who we are.

When we know that God created us for a reason, and we understand that our identity is found in Him and being created in His image, we can live from that place of purpose every day, no matter where we are on the journey. When it doesn't look how we thought it would, we can trust in who God is and who He made us to be. This trust in God and in the identity He gave us can surpass the longing we have for things to look how we expected.

We can be in the middle of an epic failure, but if we are confident in our identity as a child of God, we can move forward with passionate purpose in our next step. We know who our Father is, and we know He is always, always in the process of redeeming.

That's where the purpose is.

It's not in the mystical calling, but it's in who God is and who we are in Him. Purpose isn't something to achieve. It's part of our identity, and we don't get to claim that we found it. God freely gives it.

I wanted my calling to fulfill all of these dreams and hopes I had for the future, when actually, God was ready to fill them with Himself on the journey. In the process, there is purpose. It's not only at the top of the mountain. It's in every step along the way.

When I think back to our long hikes in Colorado, I don't just remember the mountain top moment. I think back and laugh about how we stumbled around on the dark trail in the early hours of the morning and how my husband had to hold my hand because the Lord blessed him with better vision. I remember watching the sunrise through the trees as we hiked, the early golden hour light shifting around us, as we shed layer after layer while the temperatures rose with the sun.

purpose in the process

I remember the break we took, sitting on rocks, applying more sunscreen, staring at the path behind us and the long way we had already come but knowing we still had a long way to go. I think about the first false summit and all the laughter and disappointment it brought when our bodies were screaming, "It would be a great time to take a break"...but we kept hiking.

I think about the satisfying view from the top and trying to catch my breath, but I also think about how small it made me feel. Even then, on top of a 14,000-foot mountain, I still couldn't see the full picture that God could see. It reminds me of how great and powerful He is and how the best way to follow Him is to keep moving forward and to keep pressing on, even though my understanding would always be limited. I've found freedom in being a limited human and trusting in an unlimited God.

When we start to think and believe we don't have a purpose, in any season, what we're really saying is we don't believe God is doing something in and through us. But He is.

Nothing disqualifies us from being used and loved by God, and we have to believe that no matter where we find ourselves, God is at work. Believing that means you believe God can use you and that you know who God is and who you are.

We don't usually get to see the full picture, but we can trust in a God who does. To us, it might look like we are nowhere near where we expected to be. But God is ready to meet us with renewal and fulfillment.

He doesn't ask us to see or know the full picture, He just

how much more?

invites us to take the next step, and He will show us the way. He reveals to us just enough as we journey with Him. He's faithful to fulfill His promises and constant in His love and kindness along the way. He's inviting you into purpose right now through identity in Him saying, "Come; follow me."

CHAPTER 11

when you start to move

When you start listening to God's voice, He might grab you by the shoulders, shake you, and ask you to do something you don't want to do.

The classic Biblical example of this is when God asked Jonah to go to Nineveh. When Jonah didn't go, he ended up redirected by God into the belly of a fish.

The goodness of God is never in question, but sometimes, in the same way, you have frustrating experiences and come into conflict with other people, you might have moments that feel that way with God.

God still speaks to us today in a variety of ways, and when we aren't listening, He knows how to get a hold of us and redirect us.

He always has a plan that is better and more beautiful than we could ever imagine. But that doesn't mean we are always going to want to hear everything He has to say. I imagine this was how Jonah felt when God asked him to go to minister to the people he found to be the most difficult, in a place He had no intention of going to.

how much more?

At times, our desires can start to become a distraction and prevent us from hearing from God. This is why we have to go to God with all of the things we want and allow God to bring them into alignment with His plans and purpose for our lives.

Have you ever wanted something more than anything? At times, I have been so convinced that if I could just have exactly what I wanted, everything else would fall into place.

When I believe that in my mind, my wanting is becoming an idol that is taking a place and position over my life that is greater than God. I need to let that longing drive me toward God and let that passionate longing be fulfilled and used by my Creator for His purposes. God can and will use it, but I have to surrender it to Him first.

After moving across the country, I felt like I knew what I wanted. I thought everything I wanted was good and would glorify God, and I spent most of my time praying and negotiating with God because what I wanted was good, and I knew He could provide it. Entering into negotiations with God isn't always the best idea, and I take comfort in reading my Bible and knowing I'm not the only one who has tried to do it.

God was trying to speak to me about the dream He had for my life and for that season, and it was different from my dream. But I wasn't listening. Instead, I was telling God about what I wanted and trying to tell Him that it was better than what He wanted for me. Have you ever done this?

When I did that, I was really choosing not to believe that God had a better plan than mine, and the disappointment we

when you start to move

so often feel is because we aren't choosing to trust His way over ours. Our choices to not obey God when He calls result in consequences, but I'm so grateful He will continuously call us and redirect us when we need it (even if it is into the belly of a giant fish).

You might think you have found the greatest solution to your disappointment or discontent. But God might be pointing you in the opposite direction. Maybe He's pointing you in a direction that doesn't make any sense to you.

One day, God grabbed a hold of me and spoke to me in a way He knew I couldn't ignore, to redirect me away from what I thought I wanted and toward what He wanted for me. I still remember sitting at the counter with my husband that morning, clutching a cup of coffee in my hands, trying to explain that I felt like God was pointing me in the wrong direction. He had been so clear to me that I felt like I couldn't fight it anymore. I knew it was God who was directing me, but at that moment, the direction felt completely opposite to where I felt I should have been going.

I had been praying for what I wanted every day, but I finally shifted my attitude and decided to admit I didn't know if what I wanted was the best thing. If you don't want to settle for something that isn't God's will and way for you, start to pray for the perfect will of the Father.

I specifically prayed in my journal and asked God to move. I asked Him to walk with me through the potential disappointment and to comfort me as He led me down this path that didn't make any sense to me. I repented for putting my desires before

how much more?

His desires, and I asked Him to move. I surrendered.

Then, God moved.

Through more conversations and encouragement, I started to see that God was moving in my current circumstances in ways I never would have seen as possible. It felt like a nonsensical route, and it wasn't direct or easy, but it was somehow better, just like He promised it would be.

When I chose to surrender those desires that were so prominent in my thoughts and so persistent in my day-to-day life, it still hurt a little bit. I was still hesitant, and it wasn't an immediate transformation into sudden joy and contentment.

Instead, it was feeling that deep longing for more in my soul and then giving it up to God, again and again, trusting He knew it was there. If He knew my longing, He would be willing to move and take action to fulfill it through Himself or through His plan for my life.

He knows you. He knows what you want, your deepest longings and greatest hopes and dreams, the things that make your heart cry out for more. He is loving and kind in immeasurable ways.

He is going to move. He is going to put into motion a plan for your life, and He is going to take those desires and longings and use them to direct you on the supernatural path He has for you.

He has a purpose for the things you want. He is going to bring both transformation and fulfillment.

when you start to move

A lot like walking on water, you can trust Him even when you can't see the full picture and even when you feel like He is leading you in a way that doesn't make sense. You can fix your eyes on Jesus and not look at your feet as much. Lock eyes with Him and trust that what seems illogical to you, makes perfect sense with faith.

If you are concerned about how you are going to get where you're going, you might start to sink. But when you look to God with trust that He will overcome any impossibility, you can walk boldly in faith and trust.

You can take a step that doesn't make sense, and when you start to move, you can trust that God will move too.

CHAPTER 12

watching from a window

If you're like me, you might find yourself trying to want what other people want for you. It's easy to want your path to look like someone else's, but the reality is, it never was and it never will be.

Trying to do what other people want for you will only confuse you. You can't try to become what God wants for someone else, and God won't give away what He has for you to someone else.

I spent a lot of time trying to want what other people wanted for me. It only became confusing and discouraging, and God doesn't want either of those things for us. Confusion and distractions can pull you away from God and away from His plan for you.

To stay focused on God and what He specifically wants to give you, you have to have an increased awareness of how you're uniquely wired. This means spending less time and energy on what other people might want for you and more time in an intimate space with God, allowing Him to speak into your life.

It's easy to seek the approval of other people and to allow

others' wants or goals for us to distract us from God's wants and goals for us.

If you're wondering if this is something you're struggling with, just consider how often you think about other people and what they think of you. When you're making a decision, how much weight do you give to outside opinions or expectations? Are you focused on honoring and glorifying God, or are you wondering if you will disappoint someone or if you will make someone else uncomfortable?

I'm going to let you in on a little secret...

You're going to disappoint people.

It might not be intentional, but someone might give you advice and tell you what they want for you. Maybe they really hope you'll consider grad school. Maybe they think your career choice should be different. Maybe they have some insights to offer on your dating life. Good, godly wisdom is always welcome, but at times, you might have to choose obedience to God and what He wants for your life over what other people want for you or even what you want for yourself.

Right after I got married, I had some people who told me that it was my chance to explore and travel the world and I would never get another shot unless I took it now. Others were happy to share their conviction that I would get to travel later, so I should settle into being a wife and embrace a more traditionally feminine role in my marriage.

It wasn't really important for me to choose one or the other. It was really important for me to lean into God, to see how He uniquely made me, and to allow Him to direct my life.

God has given you unique desires, and a unique calling, and a unique path to accomplish His purposes for you. It isn't going to look exactly like anyone else's, and that's a *good* thing. He made you different.

You have gifts and talents, a unique personality, and dreams for your life. You are going to want things that are different from what other people want. God made us all different, wanting different things because He has different roles for each of us in the Kingdom. It's not a one-size- fits-all kind of thing.

I want to give you permission to want things in life, even if they are unexpected, scary, or different from what the people around you want for you. You might surprise people with what you want, and honestly, you might even surprise yourself. I hope you do because that's a hint that it's God who is stirring something new in you.

He created us before He even created the world. "Long before he laid down earth's foundations, he had us in mind" (Ephesians 1:4 MSG). Some of our hopes and desires have been around for a very long time, and He doesn't want us to miss those either. Ephesians 2:10 in the New Living Translation says, "For we are God's masterpiece. He has created us anew in Christ Jesus, so we can do the good things he planned for us long ago."

That dream you have had forever? It *matters*.

There will always be people who offer opinions and judgments while watching us from the sidelines. They aren't even playing the game.

In the Bible, people were watching from the window.

> *As the ark of the covenant of the Lord was entering the City of David, Michal daughter of Saul watched from a window. And when she saw King David dancing and celebrating, she despised him in her heart.*
> 1 Chronicles 15:29, NIV

This verse caught me off guard. Why does Michal despise David?

He's joyful, he's celebrating, and he's worshiping God.

She's watching, and she is judging what he's doing.

Michal was offended and upset by David's actions, but he was doing exactly what he should have been doing. The ark of the covenant was a physical representation of God's presence in the Old Testament. David was in the presence of the Lord and He was celebrating.

Michal didn't want David to be acting like he was, and she took offense and despised him for it. She stood by watching from the window as the presence of God entered the space.

At first, this verse surprised me, but it also felt oddly familiar to me.

If your dream or desire puts you in the presence of the Lord,

watching from a window

don't let the people watching from the window stop you from moving and rejoicing in it. People are always going to have an opinion about what we are doing and what we are pursuing, but God is the only One who really knows what is within our hearts and what is behind our actions.

I'm not saying you can do whatever you want. Don't believe the lie that you will always have good desires or let just any desire lead your life. Instead, take them all to the Father. Tell Him with open hands and a heart of surrender about what you want and ask Him about what *He* wants. Watch what He does.

Some of your desires are from Him, and He puts them on your heart because He has a specific plan for you and for your life. When you lean into that, you will feel the most like who God originally designed you to be. When you pursue those longings, when you act on what the Spirit is prompting you to do, you'll end up in the presence of God—joyful and delighting in Him. And it's okay if that makes someone else uncomfortable. What matters is that you are being obedient to God.

Let your desires come into alignment with God's desires for your life. Ask Him for those desires He had for you at the very beginning. Don't look at what other people want for you. Also, don't immediately trust what you think you want for yourself.

Go to God every time, sit at His feet, and wait. Listen and let Him plant what He wants for you in you. Tell Him what you want and entrust that to Him. He is going to give you more than you could ever imagine. He's just that good.

You might want some crazy and unexpected things. Some

how much more?

things will feel too soon or too late, and you will disappoint some people along the way when you take chances. Not everyone will understand what you're doing, but they don't need to.

Maybe Michal thought David looked foolish, but David was obedient to what God wanted. David wasn't focused on what Michal wanted from him, and if he had been, he would have missed out on a moment of delighting in the Father and bringing glory to God. I don't want you to miss that.

When you're obedient and willing to do what God wants for you, you'll find yourself right in the center of the presence of God, dancing and celebrating, and you won't notice if anyone is watching.

CHAPTER 13

his promise is his presence

God created us as people who want things. We are limited in other areas like knowledge, time, and abilities. We get hungry and tired. But we can always want more. If you're like me, you might think it can be selfish or wrong to want more for your life. But what if God made you want more on purpose? What if there is an intentional design behind your desire for more in your life?

It can feel like you should want less. It can feel ungodly or unholy to want more from life. It might feel like you should hide or disguise the hopes and dreams you have for your life because they feel too detailed or too far away. Maybe you don't want to be thought of as materialistic or maybe you've felt shame for wanting more.

If you run away and hide from the things you want or daydream about, it will always lead you farther from God rather than closer to Him. God created us to want things, and the things we want can direct us toward Him.

Misplaced desire is destructive, but healthy desire, when

surrendered to a good and powerful God, is beautiful. It gives you direction and purpose and devotion, and the Holy Spirit brings both transformation and fulfillment to it.

He alone can fulfill every longing you have. He made us to long for more of Him, and He's always willing to pour out more of His Spirit on us. All of the other big hopes, dreams, and desires you have for your life will ultimately be met by God. Whether He gives you the dream or not, His promise is His presence.

When you face a difficulty that's bigger than you—the kind of thing that knocks you out of your false perception of control and makes you turn to God in desperation and longing—you need to know that He is bigger than everything.

The first time I stepped foot into what we would call a "charismatic" church, I was terrified. Don't get too caught up on the denomination thing. The church was made for unity, and I have loved, learned, and worshiped Jesus with people of all different backgrounds. That's how it should be.

At this particular church, I witnessed something I had never seen before.

I walked in with limited knowledge of the Bible, limited experience with God, and no experience in pursuing Him in a charismatic context.

Here, people were raising their hands eagerly and with urgency. They were crying out to God, and they sang and spoke words that didn't come straight from the lyrics on the screen. Instead, they were communing with their Father in this eager and intimate way I had never seen before, and I didn't understand.

I left thinking it was really weird, but also thinking, "I don't have that relationship with God, so I shouldn't go back."

Later on, I sat with a guy in the lobby of my dorm talking about church. I told him I had never seen people worship like that before, and I had never seen anything like that church before. It was weird and a little scary. How do I know what they're doing is real and that it's okay?

He looked at me and said, "I think you keep going until you find out for yourself."

And that is how I picked my church in college: with the help of one pivotal conversation with the man who would become my husband in a few years. Isn't God funny?

So I kept going, and I found out for myself.

It turned out I had what these people had, but it was misplaced.

Every week, in that little church, in Indiana, on a Sunday night, I would learn to worship God by watching other people worship Him. I saw it all over their faces, in their body language, as they fell to their knees, in the way they would lean their faces up toward heaven and hold up a hand as if they could get closer to God. They were all full of desire. They wanted more.

Their desire was pure, and in those moments, it was fixed on Jesus. It was fixed on His power, authority, peace, and grace.

how much more?

They would spend the hour of worship crying out to God how much they wanted and needed Him. Then they would shuffle to their chairs, sit down, fold their hands, and a peace would settle over the room. Even before I experienced God in this way myself, I understood that when this room of people asked God for more, He delivered it.

This is a picture of what I want my desires and longings to look like.

In that church, people walked in wanting all sorts of different things. Maybe they walked in wanting to see a family member get healed. Maybe they walked in wanting a breakthrough in an area of their life. Maybe they needed a change in their finances. Maybe they wanted to see God move in a dream they'd carried with them for their entire life.

All of those things they wanted came in the door with them, but when they cried out for more of God, and He gave them more of His presence, something changed. I still can't describe it with words, but if you've experienced it before you recognize this peace that surpasses all understanding (Philippians 4:6).

John Piper wrote, "We desire the wrong things, and we desire the right things in the wrong way. And both are deadly—like eating pleasant poison".[3]

The things we want can lead us away from God, but they're also an opportunity to grow closer to Him. Even the specific, hopeful things we want like a house with a front porch swing or to travel in the Swiss Alps.

his promise is his presence

Often, God will give you that exact specific thing you pray for because He's just that good. Other times, He will meet you with His presence, and you'll walk out the front door of the church, seemingly the same way you walked in, though, between you and God, something shifted.

An example in the Bible that I love of a specific desire being met by God is in 1 Samuel 18. David and Michal fell in love, and he wanted to marry her. Have you ever prayed that "Please let this be my future spouse" prayer after a perfect first date?

Michal was Saul's daughter, and when God saw David and Michal's love, He made a way for David to be with her. God supernaturally empowered David to exceed Saul's tall order of wanting a hundred Philistines in order for David to marry Michal. God even allowed David to return with two hundred—double what was asked of him—and He made a way for David to marry Michal.

At times, I want a specific thing. God loves marriage, and it brings Him glory. He made a way for David to be with Michal. Sometimes, God delights in giving you things you want, just because. When you receive a small thing or a big thing from God, it often results in delighting in Him. I can picture David rejoicing as he comes home with double what was asked of him, knowing he would get to be with Michal.

In that moment, David grew closer to God. The result was David wanting even more of God—more of His power, more of His presence, more of His hand on his life, more opportunities to glorify Him.

how much more?

It starts with going to God.

When I say go to God and give what you want to Him, I mean it. The thing is, you have to already be certain that God is a God who can powerfully change things. You have to be certain that He is a God who works miracles—One who has power and authority in your life. Otherwise, why would you go to Him?

We have to believe in the power of prayer. We have to know that the power of prayer is real and that prayer changes everything. That's where the transformation in our hearts, minds, and spirits happens. This kind of prayer depends on us knowing that we have a real relationship with God, that He knows us, and that we know Him. We must know that we can depend on Him to be a good Father—we can depend on Him to transform us.

You might really want something and not get it. It happens. I've found that when it does happen, it is really, truly, because God has something better in store for us. Not in the cliché way but in a profound, supernatural way.

I don't want you to miss out on the adventure God is inviting you into by choosing to settle for what seems comfortable and "good enough." I don't want you to miss out on the greater thing God is doing because you're ready to settle for what you want in your limited human moments.

God wants you to take the miraculous route with Him. He wants to move beyond your limitations in a way only He can. He can use what you want to lead you in an extraordinary direction.

his promise is his presence

He can give you what you want as easily as He gave David double the amount of Philistines needed. The even better thing is His presence with you in the waiting, in the battle, and as you chase after God-given dreams together.

Surrender what you want to God in prayer and invite His Spirit into it. Ask Him to use it for His Kingdom and for His glory. Ask Him to transform it, and be confident that He will. Ask Him to allow your greatest hopes and dreams to draw you closer to Him.

Transformation isn't always immediate—it's often slow and steady.

One day, you might be worried about a specific thing you want or you might feel like you need to have success in a specific area. Maybe you feel desperate or even hopeless. The next day, you might be trusting in the certainty that God is who He says He is, and He never makes a promise that He doesn't keep.

He is always faithful to bring the harvest, so you don't have to worry about the harvest. Instead, you can just continue to sow faithfully. The sowing becomes easier out of faithful obedience when you trust the One who brings the harvest and can see the Kingdom impact as more important than your personal impact.

I want to write—it's one of my desires. Before I write, I ask God to use it for His glory. When I surrender that desire to Him, He can use it in ways I never would have imagined and go far beyond what I would have expected. As a result, I grew more in love with Jesus than when I started.

how much more?

When you surrender what you want to Him, He can use it for His glory. And it's fun! I love the opportunities, connections, and projects I've been a part of as I've surrendered to God my desire to write. I even smile thinking about it now because He's already done so much more than I ever thought could be done through me simply wanting to write.

He will do this for you.

Go to Him, not with shame, guilt, or fear, but go to your good, powerful Father and ask Him for transformation. He knows your heart, and He knows what you want. He made you, but He wants to hear about it from you. He's a relational God, and He's inviting you into a conversation. Tell Him about what you want, and then, entrust those things to Him. Every dream, every hope, every little wish.

Acknowledge that He is the one who made you, the one who knows you inside out, and He is the one who can transform what you want and use those things for His glory and for your good (Romans 8:28).

Allow His Spirit to illuminate how those things you want could be redirected for a greater purpose. How could this desire in you be used by God? For His people? For His Kingdom?

I know it can be, and I can't wait for you to watch as God uses what you thought didn't matter. I can't wait for you to see God pull it out and use it to do something truly beautiful. When He does, you'll want even more of God.

It's not wrong to want something, but it will lead to frustration and disappointment if you don't give over those things you want to God and trust Him. When you do trust Him, He'll bring the renewal, accomplish the work, and you'll be full of purpose and joy. As you experience more of Him, I hope someone else is around to notice—maybe a confused college kid in a church pew. I hope they see the purpose and joy in you and start to want more of God for themselves too.

CHAPTER 14

prepare your table

I've always been susceptible to pneumonia, and I had it multiple times as a kid. When I got pneumonia again as an adult, I noticed it felt totally different.

I was having trouble doing basic things, and I was getting tired so easily. I needed a lot of help. I was suddenly incapable of taking care of myself, and I had to rely on other people.

When I was a kid, I remember being at home with my parents who would check in on me when I was up at night coughing. I remember them bringing me food and making me drink and eat things to help me get better. I remember them taking me to the doctor and reminding me to take my medicine at the right times. As a kid, it felt easy and natural to need help and to receive it. As an adult, it felt awkward.

As a kid, you don't notice how much people help you because you are used to needing and receiving help. You can't tie your own shoes, you need someone to cook for you, and you don't know left from right. You need someone telling you where you need to be when you need to be there and you're willing to hop in the minivan full of trust, knowing they're going to get you where you need to go.

how much more?

You aren't concerned with meeting your own needs because you're being taken care of by someone else who you can trust and rely on for all of those things.

It's fair to say that kids are needy.

When I got sick as an adult, that's how I felt again, and I wasn't used to it. I needed a lot from other people, and I had to say *yes* and receive it because I didn't have a better option. Because I was incapable of meeting my own needs, I became incredibly willing to receive from other people. I needed help, so I eagerly welcomed it and received it. The circumstances forced me into a posture of receiving.

There is such a difference in the posture you have in receiving as a kid versus as an adult. As a kid, you're eager to receive. You trust the people who take care of you. You don't shy away from asking for help when you need it. You want things and you ask for things, sometimes even crazy things because of that innocent trust you place in your parents or authority figures.

As an adult, you might be a bit more prideful regarding your ability to take care of yourself and less willing to admit you need help. Receiving help, guidance, or even a gift can become a strange and uncomfortable thing.

Kids just receive. They ask for help when they need it—often repeatedly. They're super capable of admitting they need help, and they will keep telling you how they feel, openly and honestly, until you help them. I think back to my babysitting days and the constant, "I'm hungry" or "I'm bored." They aren't shy about what they want or need.

prepare your table

Kids don't think they know better, and they're not ashamed of it either. They're open, receptive, and admittedly unaware of what to do next, how to do it, or what steps to take to get there.

As an adult, you might become shy or awkward about your wants or needs. The expectation shifts from being eager to receive help or new knowledge, to politely refusing help and adopting a "do it yourself" attitude.

Maybe you're nervous to say yes when someone offers to do something for you because you might have to admit you can't do it for yourself.

Maybe it feels uncomfortable to talk to God about what you want and need because you're so used to how the world tells us we should be self-sufficient.

Jesus invites us to receive the Kingdom like kids, and that is an invitation to let go of our futile attempt at self-sufficiency and to depend on Him instead. You can be eager to receive, without reservations about needing help, and open to the fact that you can't take care of yourself, but you know someone who can.

When it comes to your dreams and hopes, maybe receiving them starts with recognizing that God knows you better, and He can give you more than what you want for yourself. John Ortberg writes, "What if the real reason we feel like we never have enough is that God is not yet finished giving? The unlimited neediness of the soul matches the unlimited grace of God."[4]

You can't get there on your own. Being dependent on Him

brings freedom. There isn't any pressure for you to accomplish what He calls you to on your own. Instead, He's faithful and He will do it (1 Thessalonians 5:24). You can depend on Him. God is going to get you where you need to go.

You can find freedom accepting things you don't understand and maybe you never will. You can still move in the Spirit with trusting obedience and hopeful anticipation. God will keep His promises to you.

There's something really special about this posture of dependency, having more trust, and having more capability to easily receive. It can feel uncomfortable to recognize our need for God and our lack of self-sufficiency. But, it's an invitation from Him to show up, to give Him what we want, and to trust Him to accomplish it.

To do this, we don't have to be strong, powerful, certain, or even put together. We just have to be sons and daughters. We have to receive like kids. Actually, the Scripture says His power is made perfect in our weakness (2 Corinthians 12:9). So if you're showing up a little afraid, uncertain, or messy, it's perfectly okay.

It's when you show up with weaknesses, turn to your Father, and ask Him to *be* a Father to you, that Heaven invades earth.

Posturing yourself like a son or daughter means having open receptivity—that trusting, dependent attitude that says, *I need you, God. I can't do this without you.*

But it also means you have to ask.

prepare your table

When you are postured as a son or daughter, asking God for the desires of our hearts should be easy. If asking God for your miracle feels clunky, hard, and awkward, that is okay. It takes practice and time. More than anything, asking is a representation of what is going on in your heart.

If I don't feel comfortable asking my parents to provide for me, do I really trust them to deliver? If I don't feel comfortable asking my parents for a gift, do I know they love me and that they would do everything they can to give generously to me?

I grew up with a family I could fall back on. This has been a huge blessing in my life, and I know it isn't the case for everyone. Whenever I was anxious about a difficult situation or a risk I wanted to take, one thing that always gave me peace of mind was my parents. I knew they would be there for me to fall back on if I needed them.

I wish I could have told you I felt the same way about God. Now, God is better than a fallback plan. He makes the best first plan. When you're postured in a healthy dependency on God and His Spirit, asking becomes easy, natural, and your first response. When you're postured in self-sufficiency, it feels awkward and prideful, like how you might feel needing to call your parents and ask for their help as a grown adult.

The posture, "I tried my best on my own, and I couldn't do it, and now I desperately need you because I can't do it myself," is a last resort out of desperation and defeated pride. In this posture, asking is filled with shame.

It is wonderful to desperately need God, but you don't need to

how much more?

feel ashamed or uncomfortable about receiving all that He has for you.

One can compare it to Christmas morning.

When I was a kid, my favorite Christmas morning tradition was when my dad made breakfast. Before we woke, my mom would set the dining room table with fancy dinnerware and these little Santa Claus napkin holders. My dad would be in his Christmas-themed pajamas, sipping coffee in the kitchen, while every burner on the stove was full of breakfast food.

My parents were incredible gift-givers, and they still are. They are great at both giving us surprises and giving us what we ask for, and that is just like the heart of God. When I was in high school, I was in that "too cool for everything" stage and was almost too cool for Christmas. But I still nonchalantly asked my parents for a pair of sparkly Ugg boots in the color purple. They were just as ridiculous as they sounded.

Those shoes were the most sought-after gift that year, and I just knew everyone would be rolling up to school with them after Christmas break. I asked my parents for purple, specifically, knowing that no one else would have purple, and that would be my way of fitting in but still standing out.

A few days before Christmas, my little sister pulled me aside and let me know I shouldn't get my hopes up because she saw my mom ordering a pair of those shoes in black. Black! I couldn't believe it. The last thing I wanted was a boring pair of black shoes, but I prepared myself for Christmas morning, ready to appear grateful when I knew those shoes would sit in

prepare your table

the back of my closet in their box for the next year.

In this metaphor, she represents all of those people who tell us to lower our expectations because what if God doesn't do what He says He will? What if God isn't really all that good? Let's be grateful for the black shoes. I'm preparing you for your own good, okay?

Christmas morning rolled around, and I pulled the shoe-shaped box from beneath the tree with all eyes on me. I was ready to open my gift, preparing myself to pretend it was what I wanted, even though I knew I would be disappointed.

I tore off the wrapping paper, opened the shoebox, and my jaw dropped as the most perfect (and hideous, I'll now add) pair of sparkly purple shoes were in front of me. I pulled them right on, and my family laughed and joked about how they had wanted me to be surprised. My little sister had made it that much sweeter by making me think I wouldn't get what I wanted.

I wore them with my pajamas all day, and, at the breakfast table, my family ate, laughed, and enjoyed being with one another. When I look back on that experience, I remember how good the gift was. I remember how much joy it brought to me, and I remember how eager I was to wear those shoes that Monday after Christmas break—to show my friends who all had the same shoes, but not in purple.

Even more, I think about how sweet it was to watch my family eagerly give me the gift I wanted. They were so delighted and filled with joy to give me what I wanted, even though, I'm

how much more?

sure; my parents thought those shoes were ridiculous. They wanted to see my happiness. Remembering that experience as an adult, all I can think about is how much my family loves me.

Positioning yourself like a son or daughter in the Kingdom of God means trusting that God knows what you want, even the small details, like the color. He knows what you want, and He knows what you need. He can fulfill all of those things, and here's the key notion: He wants to.

That doesn't mean you will get everything you want, but I do know He is a giver of good gifts, and He wants to give to you (Matthew 7:11). Also, He wants the same laughter and joy I remember from Christmas morning. He wants the communion of sitting at the breakfast table, delighting in giving and receiving.

Let's ask and receive like kids with that open receptivity and trusting, dependent attitude saying, "We need you, God. We want your Kingdom. We don't know a better way. We need your way." And when we ask, let's not sit and wonder if He can do it, but let's prepare a table to commune with Him when He does.

CHAPTER 15

my miracle is your miracle

Do you know that feeling when you watch someone receive what you wanted before you do, or maybe get exactly what you wanted when you might never get it? I've been on both sides of that before.

My husband and I were the classic Christian college love story. We met during our freshman year, we were dating by our sophomore year, engaged by our junior year, and we even graduated a semester early, so we were the first ones to be married and off into the "real world."

I wasn't the classic, Christian college student though. At least, I didn't think of myself that way. I didn't think a lot about my wedding, I didn't think a lot about meeting anyone, and I definitely didn't think about meeting my future husband at college.

When I arrived on campus in the fall of my freshman year and witnessed the "freshman frenzy," in which the new students quickly pair off and start relationships, I was surprised that so many people expected to meet their future spouses in their first

how much more?

semester of college. Then, I ended up being "that girl."

A lot of women my age dreamed about meeting their future husbands at school. Now, knowing what I know, I don't blame them for that. When you attend a Christian college, it's a great time to meet someone, and it's a great opportunity to find someone who is like-minded. You can easily find someone with whom you have a lot in common, and you already have all of those shared college experiences.

The "ring by spring" trend makes a lot of sense to me because there were so many incredible people on our campus who were able to form incredible relationships and say, "Hey! Let's do this together for life!"

As a young, often self-centered college student, I didn't realize the position I was in when I met my husband. My relationship was overly romantic. We were, and are, kind of over-the-top in love with each other.

I love to celebrate, I love love, and my husband is absolutely incredible at making me feel special. If I had an early meeting in the student center, I would walk by the campus coffee shop, and the barista would pass me a coffee that was already paid for and waiting for me as a surprise. People would look at me and say, "How cute!"

What I didn't realize at the time was that I was receiving the attention and affection that so many of my peers were praying for.

I would rush out of my dorm room to go on extravagant dates

my miracle is your miracle

and come back gushing with stories of this incredible guy, forgetting to realize there were single women in the room who would give anything in the world to have what I had.

When I went abroad, my boyfriend (at the time) shocked me and everyone who knew me when he showed up one Friday afternoon in Ireland to surprise me and get down on one knee. I was the first one in my close friend group to get engaged, and I was so excited and so focused on the joy of this gift God had given me that I forgot to turn my head to the side and see the people who were hurting beside me.

Maybe that feels familiar to you, being the one who unexpectedly received something that so many people sought after. Or, maybe you know what it feels like to watch someone receive the very thing you have been praying for fervently on your knees every day.

Have you ever asked God, "Why them; why not me?" Or, have you ever thought to yourself, "She didn't even pray for it."

One time, I had been praying every day for the same thing and working hard to move towards accomplishing it in my daily life. I was both taking action and partnering with the Holy Spirit, but I still hadn't seen my miracle. Do you know the feeling?

You know that thing you think about all of the time—the thing that you want so badly, you can't stop thinking about it? It's the kind of thing that fills your spirit with longing and your mind with daydreams. You spend so much time yearning for it, chasing after it, and praying to God for it.

how much more?

Do you know the feeling when someone who hasn't ever really wanted that thing, at least not as much as you wanted it, gets it?

Maybe it was a friend accidentally getting pregnant when you struggle with infertility or a friend finding her partner for life when you've been praying for a relationship. She said she wasn't interested in dating! Or, maybe someone else received an opportunity or a job offer that was unexpected, yet perfect, and it was what you'd wanted and had been working toward.

I watched a friend get exactly what I wanted before me. I was praying for it, and her success and receipt of what I wanted snuck up on her and took her by surprise. I wanted what she had so badly, but I prayed and prayed, asking God, by His power, to help me overcome the longing.

I was nervous to even talk to her because I assumed wrongly that if she got it, that meant I didn't. In reality, God will never give what He has for you to someone else. You can always celebrate someone else receiving something from God because that never means He isn't going to give to you.

The conversation I had with my friend wasn't at all what I thought it would be.

If you'd heard her, you might have been shocked like I was. I thought she was going to tell me how deserving she was of what she had received, how she was so awesome, incredible, and gifted, and how she was the most capable human for this assignment.

Instead, she gave complete and total glory to God. She told

my miracle is your miracle

me all about the miraculous way God dropped this surprising gift in her life at a time she didn't predict or expect and how redemptive His work was in it. I was so encouraged and so moved by the power of God, while she told me her story, that I left the conversation feeling so far from the disappointment I had initially felt.

I felt like worshiping Jesus instead.

I was suddenly so thankful God decided to use her in this new way, and I was so amazed at how He was at work in her life. She wasn't deserving of it, and she was the first person to say that, but because He is so, so good, He wanted to do this for her and redeem a part of her story by giving her this beautiful gift.

I suddenly saw the story God was writing and how much bigger it was than what I wanted. I saw the glory of God in her life, and I just wanted to marvel at it instead of thinking about how I felt slighted or overlooked because I didn't have what I wanted yet.

I was more certain of the goodness of God than I was before I saw her miracle. When you see God do more in someone else's life, let it be a reminder He can do more in your life too. Just because He hasn't answered your prayer doesn't mean He won't.

God is the One who assigns us to different seasons, ministries, opportunities, and relationships, and He chooses who He positions where and when.

Seeing God give generously to someone else can give you the

confidence to know that He can and will keep His promises to you too. To have confidence in His promises to us, we need to be familiar with them. When we are familiar with God's Word, we can echo, "I desire to do your will, my God; your law is within my heart" (Psalm 40:8 NIV).

When you know His heart for you, you can focus on your relationship with Him free from comparison. Other people might get what you want before you do. Sometimes, you're the friend getting married and falling in love first. And other times you're on your knees in tears begging God to move and work a miracle.

In both places, He sees you. In both positions, He is good.

We aren't entitled to get everything we want from God, but He is a Father who desires to give us every good thing (Psalm 84:11).

What if we decided to share our miracles? When I get my miracle, I want to share it with you and tell you that God is good, He is capable, and He sees you. I believe your miracle is coming soon.

And when you get your miracle first, I want to praise God for being a good and kind Father who gives so generously. His giving to you gives me hope that He is capable of giving to me too.

CHAPTER 16

met by authority

When you are faced with disappointment, you need to look at the expectations you have for your life and compare them to the Word of God. It can be intimidating to do this because you might be afraid of discovering that God's promises are different from your expectations.

What if you found that God could not fulfill all of the desires and longings you had? What if your expectations are out of place, but your loyalty lies with them, and what if, in the end, you find out that God isn't truly good?

What I discovered was entirely the opposite.

A lot of us have decided to dismiss the things we want before we take a good, long look at them. Somehow, we've stumbled into the thought process that wanting more is wrong, bad, or evil. Not everything we want is good, but God can use all of it.

Some of those things we want were actually placed in our life by God Himself, and that longing and hunger for change are what pushes us into places we wouldn't dare walk before—places where we are forced into dependency on the Holy Spirit because of the impossibility of a circumstance or a situation

how much more?

cannot be conquered without Him.

Understanding my desires, God's desires, and promises that weren't yet fulfilled by God, brought me into a realization that the fulfillment of those things was all dependent on one thing: Did I believe God was who He said He was? You probably want more for yourself, but do you believe that God wants more for you?

If God is who He says He is, then He has authority over all things; even the crazy things, the scary things, and the small things; even your longings, desires, dreams, and goals. Do you believe He has authority over everything you want?

As kids, we are eager to want more, even if the outcome seems impossible. Ask any kid what they want to be when they grow up, and you'll get so many creative answers. When they answer, you'll probably silently have the reasons in your mind as to why they might not end up becoming a dolphin trainer, etc.

When I was a little girl, before I was old enough to take a dance class, I wore the same ballet tutu every day for a year, dreaming of becoming a ballerina. When I was in middle school listening to authors who came and talked about their books at the library, I dreamt of a day when my name would be on a book cover, and I started to practice my signature for future book signings.

Even now, I curate Pinterest boards filled with images of renovated vans to travel the country in, the bohemian decorated houses of my dreams, and excessive photos of surreal camping

met by authority

views in the mountains.

As adults, a lot of us grow out of our dreams. We start to pick careers based on a salary, or we pick places to live based on what's practical. Sometimes we even silence and push down those dreams in our hearts because of the voices of realism, or even worse, what other people think we should do. We start to put the power in the hands of practicality or realism and dismiss the dreams that God may have placed there for a purpose.

In his book, *Start*, Jon Acuff mentions a study that found people who were dying shared a common regret. The number one thing they regretted was an unfulfilled dream, or in other words, not having the courage to do something that was true to who they really were.[5] Mary Oliver wrote, "The most regretful people on earth are those who felt the call to creative work, who felt their own creative power restive and uprising, and gave it neither power nor time."[6]

You probably don't want to become a regretful person. But you also might struggle to give certain dreams or hopes for your life attention and devotion, especially if they are easily dismissed by other people in your life.

A lot of us have heard the narrative that something we want doesn't matter. At times, the underlying statement is not just that what we want doesn't matter, but that God doesn't want it for us or that He just doesn't care about what we want.

You might start to wonder, *Is it wrong to want to become wealthy? I know I want to give above and beyond, but is it wrong to ask God for greater provision? Is it wrong to want to*

how much more?

feel purpose in work, or should I feel purpose in God alone? Is it wrong to want more friends? Should God Himself fulfill my longing for community?

Often, when I've admitted things I want, especially the ones with specific details curated in a vivid daydream, I've been met with a little bit of laughter and comments that essentially say, "But God probably doesn't want that."

So, what does God say about the dreams and desires we have for our life?

How do we avoid that horrible regret of feeling like our life is one of an unfulfilled promise?

How do we give the things we want the time and attention they deserve in our lives without letting them become idols?

Here are some things I know to be true of our God: He is a good Father, and He is always capable of fulfilling all of our dreams because all power belongs to Him (Psalm 62:11). He's also a kind and generous God, able to provide for all of our needs (Philippians 4:19). He gives us more than we deserve, and He is a God of abundance and blessing (Ephesians 3:20). He has authority over all things, which means He can give us all things (Romans 8:32).

He can fulfill all of our dreams easily but will He?

This is a complex question.

When I look to the Word of God and who God reveals Himself

to be, He loves dreams. He speaks to His people through dreams and visions. I think the dreams we have for our lives are often good gifts from God (James 1:17). We are also told that "a dream comes when there are many cares" (Ecclesiastes 5:3 NIV). Honoring the dream God has placed in your heart is a matter of stewardship, honoring the dream honors God. "If people can't see what God is doing, they stumble all over themselves; But when they attend to what he reveals, they are most blessed" (Proverbs 29:18).

God desires us to have that same spirit we had as kids when we said, "I want to be a ballet dancer!" before ever stepping foot in a dance studio.

It honors God when we ask for wild, crazy things because what we're doing is telling Him, "I believe you have authority over this, and I think you can accomplish this unrealistic or seemingly impossible thing I'm asking for." In telling Him about our crazy dreams, we show Him we have crazy faith in Him too.

At the same time, as we ask with the knowledge and recognition of God having full authority over all things, even that mountain in Matthew 17, we have to be fully surrendered to the will of God. We have to trust in His sovereign plan and know that some dreams and desires we are praying for might not even be scratching the surface of what God has in store for us. We have to have faith that His plan is better. We have to believe that, not in a "His plan is better" way, as we shrug off our dreams in disappointment but rather in a transformative way that impacts how we live and what we want.

how much more?

I haven't seen all of my craziest, wildest dreams and desires happen yet, but I still pray for them. I still declare them over myself, and when people ask me about them, I look them in the eyes and tell them those things I want out loud. I know it sounds crazy, but I also know that the things we want, when met with the authority and power of God, are possible.

I believe God created us with a longing for more, so He could use it for His glory, and ultimately, to direct us to Him. More than anything else, I go to the feet of Jesus with things I long for. He wants that. Jesus told us to go to a place of intimate prayer with the Father, "Here's what I want you to do: Find a quiet, secluded place so you won't be tempted to role-play before God. Just be there as simply and honestly as you can manage. The focus will shift from you to God, and you will begin to sense his grace" (Matthew 6:6 MSG).

When I sit at His feet, fully surrendered, I believe He takes those things I want and starts to form them into what *He* needs to fulfill His plans and purpose on earth. He wants to use them.

One of my favorite examples of this in scripture is in 1 Samuel 1 and 2. Hannah wants a baby. We are told she is in "deep anguish" (v. 10), she "weeps bitterly" (v. 10), and she is "deeply troubled" (v. 15). I love this story so much because Hannah's desire for a child is met by God's authority and generosity, and we see a shift happen in her heart and in her circumstances.

Hannah first makes the choice to turn to God. She prays, "...out of my great anguish and grief" (v. 16). I can see it. She knew God, she loved God, and God had been good to her, but she just wanted this one thing so badly that it took her focus off anything else. She was so consumed by her desire for a child that it brought her to a place of desperation, crying out to God.

Hannah's desire for a baby placed her before the throne of God, crying out to Him, in a moment of intimacy, in the midst of her desires. This moment of meeting with God is where the change happens. This is where we are invited to experience the same transformation Hannah experienced.

I don't think we are guaranteed to receive our miracle every time. I don't think we get "results" in a transactional way every time. But, I do think we will be met with our good, supernatural God every time.

Hannah leaves with, "her face no longer downcast" (v. 18). This is *before* God gives her a child when her spirit was completely transformed. God first fulfilled the desire with Himself and then He actually gave her exactly what she asked for because He is just that good. First, He did transformative work in her spirit, and *then* He answered her specific prayer and gave her the desire of her heart.

I want the longings for my life to be transformed. I want the anguish and grief to be replaced with calm contentment that only God can give.

God is constantly inviting us to partner with Him and to pray for the miraculous.

What if Hannah hadn't prayed?

What if she didn't get to be a part of asking God to fulfill her longing for a child and watching Him miraculously show up? What if she'd felt afraid and guilty about how she wanted to be a mom, so she never went to the throne of God and asked Him to move for her?

She would have really missed out on the miracle God wanted to work in her life, and she would've missed the faith and intimacy He wanted to build in her relationship with Him. She would have missed out on seeing God move on her behalf in His graciousness and kindness, and she would have missed out on a chance to witness His glory in her life. Not only that, but everyone who witnessed her miracle would have missed out on seeing God come and move with power too.

Don't feel guilty or afraid about what you want. Instead, surrender it to God, and invite His Spirit to form it into what He needs to advance the gospel and make disciples.

God has a purpose behind the things we want, and when we turn to Him with those longings, we are able to move into deeper faith and intimacy with Him. They invite us into a deeper relationship. In the same way God worked in Hannah, He can work in us. He wants to do something in our spirits first; then He can use His authority to move on our behalf too.

The focus cannot be on what God can do for us; it has to be on who God is to us.

We could pray for the same thing continuously before we see it answered, or we might be in a season where we are asking for the same thing every day, and we still haven't received our breakthrough. To be content in this, we have to have a

met by authority

right relationship with the Father—that should be fulfillment enough.

It has to be built on a deep relationship of trust and intimacy that allows us to wait, be still, and appreciate living while we wait for all the promises that are yet to come.

God is a God of abundance and blessing. He's a God who turns water into wine—He provides more than enough. He's a God who throws a party for the prodigal son with an abundant celebration and a feast. He's a God who gives eternal life freely to anyone who asks, even though all of us are undeserving of that gift. When we remember this, the truth of the gospel and the truth of who God is, all the things we want in life, are met by a God who knows, a God who gives, and most importantly, a God who already gave.

God gives more than we can imagine. Maybe you have a wild imagination or maybe you need to challenge yourself to dream bigger. Can I challenge you to not stop at the dreaming?

Oftentimes, when we are wrestling with why things aren't "going our way," it's because we aren't coming into agreement with the promises God has made us. We have access to God who has authority over all things.

When we know the truth that God has authority, we pray from that place. We know He has authority over all things and all impossibilities we might face. Because of this, we have the confidence to tackle anything in our prayers, our relationships, our careers, and in our actions.

how much more?

You aren't inconveniencing God with your wildly detailed daydreams. Don't approach Him timidly, afraid to ask for too much. He already knows the grand visions you have for your future, those floating around in your head. He knows every desire you have, He knit you together in your mother's womb, and He is fully aware of the intricacies of your longings.

We honor Him by asking for big, crazy things because in doing so we are saying we are confident as sons and daughters, and we are certain of the authority He has over all things.

His dreams for our lives are bigger than our dreams for our lives. His way is better. He is faithful.

Maybe our dying regret wouldn't be not having the courage to start pursuing our dreams, but I think it would be not asking God for what we want and allowing Him to meet it with His authority. James 4:2 says, "You do not have because you do not ask God."

Nothing is unmanageable for God. God doesn't feel inconvenienced or bothered by crazy, specific requests or the big hopes and dreams we have—the dreams so big we're afraid to admit them to our closest friends over coffee. His Spirit is nudging you gently and saying, "Come on; dream bigger. I can do anything."

Invite His Spirit into those places of longing. He's there to fulfill those longings and desires while you wait.

Are you longing for a vocation and career that glorifies God and feels purposeful? God has a need for you in the workplace,

met by authority

He has specifically equipped you and gifted you for the job He had in mind the moment He created you, and for now, He's with you while you work the drive-thru line at Starbucks.

He's equipping you, preparing you, and working in you to love His people right where you are today. He wants to give you Himself and equip you with the greatest sense of purpose you will feel in any setting, by advancing the Kingdom of God in partnership with His Spirit.

Maybe your body is sick, and you're praying for a miracle. Maybe you're waiting for your miracle, desiring a body that is functioning and working as it was originally designed. God wants to heal you—He loves to heal and restore. If it doesn't happen the moment you read these words (and I pray it does), then know He is with you.

He sent His Son to experience pain and physical hurt. He sent Him to experience death and then conquer it when He rose again. Now Jesus is seated at the right hand of the Father, His ear is turned toward you, communing with you, and He is listening to your prayers with an empathy beyond what we can understand. He knows it hurts. He is healing.

He knows your desires—even the ones you're afraid or ashamed to say out loud. I dare you to say them out loud right now, just in the quiet company of your Father. Let Him know what you want. Release them to Him, confident that they are under His authority.

Then, let Him know that more than anything, you want more of Him.

CHAPTER 17

limitations met by transformation

We live in a culture that doesn't like limitations. When I was in middle school, my sisters and I begged my dad for unlimited data, and now you probably can't even imagine what life was like before unlimited data was a thing.

We want it all, we want it fast, and we don't want to be told *no* or that we can't have something or do something. When you feel limited, it can be disappointing and frustrating.

I doubt you like feeling limited. Instead, most of us would prefer to have an abundance of choices and freedom without limits.

It can be so frustrating when you are confronted with your limitations. You are a limited human. Even with the help of all the productivity hacks in the world, you are limited in what you can accomplish in a certain amount of time and limited in how much creativity you can muster up.

You only have a certain capacity for emotion, and when you reach it you could become emotionally exhausted and drained.

how much more?

You need to rest.

When you dream big dreams, pray big prayers, and acknowledge the things you want for the future, you will be confronted with limitations. And people around you will likely remind you that you're limited too.

Growth can only happen so fast. You can only learn so much in an amount of time. You are limited in your knowledge, you are limited in your time, and you are limited in experience. There is only so much you can do.

Does this message sound familiar to you? It is one that is easy to receive with frustration and helplessness.

When there are so many things you want, but the limitations of your humanness get in the way, it can start to feel like the best thing to do is to climb back into bed first thing in the morning because you feel the weight of impossibility.

But that is when God does His best work.

When you feel the pressure of people around you asking, *"How will you do it?"* you can point to God and say, *"I don't know, but He does."*

One morning, I opened up my Bible not even thinking about my limitations. It was during a week that had been hard. It was action-packed with social events and work obligations, and my body kept telling me to rest, but I wasn't listening. What limit? Who, me? I don't have limits…

limitations met by transformation

I was reading 2 Kings 4:38-44, when I saw what God does with our human limitations.

There was a famine in the land, so the people were very limited in what they could eat. They made stew with gourds, not realizing the gourds they had were poisonous. Then, Elisha simply added flour, and God supernaturally allowed them to eat what was previously poison without any issues.

After that, a man brought twenty loaves of bread hoping to feed the people with this offering. They were concerned it was not enough for 100 men but God declared that there would be more than enough. Everyone ate, and they even had food left over.

When I read this passage, I saw people with limitations. They were in a famine. They didn't have choices. There were no options—it wasn't an abundant buffet. They just ate what they could find. They were desperate. The only thing available to them was poisonous.

Their bodies were limited, so they couldn't consume the poison. But God met their limitations with His supernatural power. He turned death into life. He took what was harmful and turned it into something nourishing and good. Thank you, Lord, for meeting our limitations with Your power.

They were limited in the food they had, and they were limited in their understanding of provision. In a famine, there isn't an abundance mindset. They were confronted with poverty all around them, so they had taken those limitations and accepted them as their norm-their reality.

how much more?

Every day, there was a mindset of "not enough" and limitation. They were limited and they were comfortable staying in those limitations: staying hungry and staying in a space where they weren't provided for or expectant for provision.

But God, who made us with limitations and who knows those limitations, came and entered into that place, where they needed more provision that wasn't harmful, and fulfilled them with more than enough.

At times, He meets the need or gives us what we want. He also fulfills those things with Himself. God isn't limited. He loves, cares, and provides for us through our limitations.

When the people in famine saw "not enough," felt hunger, and embraced the belief that they wouldn't be provided for, God took what they had with the limited amount of food and the limited expectation and belief, and He provided more than enough. He gave generously, as He always does, taking scarcity and turning it into abundance. He isn't limited by what limits us.

When you are in a position that reminds you that you are limited, instead of feeling frustrated or helpless, you can respond by turning to an unlimited God.

Fasting is a practice that allows us to be reminded of our limitations. Instead of settling into the comfortable routine of eating, choose to stay in the discomfort and sit with the reminder that you are limited. You are *hungry*.

Fasting reminds me that I am limited. When I get hungry, I get

limitations met by transformation

headaches, I get tired, and I struggle to stay focused.

I'm limited. But God isn't. Where you have a limitation, it can become an invitation for God to work a miracle—to provide and give you more of Him.

God is a God of abundance. You can embrace the limited hours you have in a day and the limited emotional and physical capacity you have—the limited gifts, talents, skills, or knowledge you have. You can embrace your limitations with God, offering all that you have as an imperfect offering, knowing that He is a God without limits.

Where you have a need or are lacking something, He sees an invitation to provide and bring abundance.

Your limitations can become empowering because you are entrusting your hopes and dreams not to your own ability or resources, but to a God without limits. He can accomplish anything. You can walk confidently in your limitations even in a time of lack while looking to God.

If you are faced with scarcity, if you're reminded of how limited you feel, if you are faced with an impossibility, know that God can give you so much more. If it feels like you're in over your head, and you don't think you have much more to offer, that might be exactly where God needs you. Elisha didn't have the power to transform, but he relied on God for His power. In our limitations, we're invited to ask God for transformation too.

CHAPTER 18

right now on earth

To know God is good, we also have to know He is who He says He is, He keeps His promises, and He is an active God. He isn't sitting up in Heaven looking down on us with a box of popcorn, watching the show.

When I was in college, I went on a mission trip. I had learned so much about God, and I was eager to get my feet on the ground and start putting what I knew to be true of my God into action by sharing it with a world in need.

We would walk around in small groups and just talk to people. The leaders of our trip were big on relationship building (a lot like Jesus) and didn't want us to jump straight into, "Do you know Jesus?"

Instead, we were taught to actually just make friends and focus on building relationships. To get to know people, understand who they were, and eventually, invite them into a conversation about who Jesus is. This was my first time on a mission trip, so I didn't have a lot of experience, but I felt like the conversations we had with people on our trip looked a lot like what I hoped my conversations looked like in daily life.

how much more?

At one point, we ran into a group from another church, and they handed us little "tickets to Heaven." They were there to accomplish the same mission as us—they wanted to tell others about Jesus. Their approach was a little different.

They started to tell us about how we needed this ticket to Heaven—how we could avoid going to Hell and get into Heaven if we confess we were sinners and repented. When they found out we were all already saved, the conversation quickly ended, and they continued to pass out tickets to Heaven to the next people.

They didn't have it all wrong, but it didn't seem like an appealing message. It didn't make me excited about following Jesus. It didn't make me want to tell other people about Him. I wrestled with this, and I still do sometimes. Evangelism, or telling people about Jesus, feels really awkward outside of the context of a relationship.

It can't all be about getting into Heaven.

We are all working our way toward it, trying to make it, but until then, we are stuck in a world full of suffering, brokenness, and disappointment.

It can feel like you are just sitting with your hopelessness and your sin as a human. When we're only focused on the hope for later, we neglect the message of hope for today that the gospel has to offer.

Dallas Willard wrote, "The work of spiritual formation in Christlikeness is the work of claiming the land of milk and honey in which we are, individually and collectively, to dwell with God"⁷

Following Jesus doesn't seem that appealing when it's all focused on getting into Heaven and staying out of Hell. That can be reductive because then we stay in the hopelessness and disappointment of the world more than we need to. It's critical to recognize the brokenness and sin in the world and to repent and move forward. But we don't need to write off the hope of Heaven as something we can only experience in the future. We can experience the goodness of God right here and now.

There is more to the story and part of the picture that is missing in the getting into Heaven message is the goodness of God and the hope He gives us immediately. The hope is not just for eternity but for our Monday mornings at the office, our hard conversations with a friend, and our biggest dreams and deepest longings.

This hope is a lot less about getting to Heaven and a lot more about bringing Heaven down.

God sent us His Son who brought Heaven to earth when He healed the sick, preached the gospel, and built a community that was opposite of what the world had in mind. The world is filled with destruction, pain, and hurt, but what God did was build, restore, and unite.

When Jesus left, He said something surprising. He said He was leaving us His Spirit because it would be better for us to have that, equipped with the power and presence of God, to do His work here in the world right now than if He stayed. Jesus gave

how much more?

us His Spirit to *bring Heaven down*. Jesus is coming back, but in the meantime, we're equipped with the Spirit to go to work.

That's a message I can get on board with. That's a message I want to share with the world.

Yes, we have all sinned and fallen short, and we need to repent and turn to God. Why? Because we can have eternal life in Heaven. We can also have access to a God with all power and authority *right now on earth* though. We get to partner with God and pray, "Heaven come!" and we get to watch it happen, right before our eyes, and transform the world.

We get to play an active role in bringing Heaven to earth. We get to pray for sick people to be healed. We get to watch broken relationships become restored. We get to watch inner peace and joy be restored in someone's life. We can see and experience the power and glory of God as we fill a space with worship and praise. God's promise to us is, as followers of Jesus in this life, that it keeps getting better.

> *And we all, who with unveiled faces contemplate the Lord's glory, are being transformed into his image with ever-increasing glory, which comes from the Lord, who is the Spirit.*
> 2 Corinthians 3:18, NIV

Have you ever been shown that image they use in vacation Bible school of you on one side and God on another with this massive deep valley in between?

If you have, then you know that the Bible teacher would

draw a huge cross that would become the bridge between you and God, and they would show you that Jesus and what was accomplished on the cross has given you access to God.

The cross becomes an image of the bridge, and it allows you to walk over to God. If you were like me when you saw this, it might have tempted you to believe that once you walk over that bridge and get access to God, you get to go to Heaven, and that's the end of the story. It's a one-time thing.

What I've learned is the real transformation and life change happens—the "ever-increasing glory" happens—when we walk over the bridge, commune with God *every day*, and turn around.

Jesus came and died to give us all authority so we could turn around and walk back and forth on that bridge multiple times every single day, carrying the presence of God back to the people and the world on the other side.

The bridge isn't one-time access so you can get to Heaven. It's a lifelong process of knowing more of God, more of His presence, more of His power, more of His peace, more of His Spirit, and bringing it to earth in your relationships, your workplace, your church, and your community.

It's like bringing your empty bucket—ready and willing to make the sacrifice of doing the work—to go and get fresh, clean water from the well, and then turning around and carrying it back to the community God has called you to.

You know you have an eternal source for life, for truth, and for

how much more?

love, and someday it won't be as hard as it is right now. But right now, He wants you to take part in the work. He invites you to help bring Heaven down into your daily life. When you do, you will experience more and more of His glory and to see more and more of Heaven here.

CHAPTER 19

with a heart for harvesting

I want to rely on the power of God. I want to take my expectations, my desires, my hopes, and my dreams, and dump them out at the feet of Jesus like I'm dumping out my laundry hamper into the washing machine and declaring, "Make it clean!" (I don't normally do laundry like that but now I might.)

But what if I don't actually trust that the washing machine will turn on, or work, or that it will get the stains out? What if I don't believe God is who He says He is, and I don't actually think He will move in my life like He does for other people?

I have always been a big dreamer. I love pursuing big, crazy dreams for my life, and I quickly become committed to a new dream. Unfortunately, that commitment often fades away because of discouragement.

Pursuing a dream or hope you have for your life can become disappointing in the process.

Maybe you thought you'd get your first clients faster, instead of spending hours coming up with new marketing ideas.

how much more?

Maybe you thought you'd experience a breakthrough in your friendships but found it took a lot of patience and a lot of work.

It is easy to become disappointed in the process of pursuing something that God has called you to, wondering why God hasn't given you a miracle yet, and if the wait will ever end. It is also possible to continue on the journey of pursuing your big hopes and dreams with a resilient faith.

Most of us probably experience both the excitement of chasing after our dreams and the hurt and let down in the process. One morning we wake up energized and ready to do the work God called us to, and we feel excited about it. The next morning, we might feel like we aren't making any progress. We might feel like we are doing everything in our control but are moving one step forward only to get pushed two steps back. Maybe we even start to doubt if we are the person to do this or if God can do it after all.

Maybe doubt sounds something like this: I don't have enough hustle to chase my dreams. I don't have enough patience to be a steadfast friend when someone is facing a challenging season that I don't know what to do with. I don't have enough endurance to love being a part of the church when it disappoints me. I don't have enough faith to keep praying for something impossible when I don't see any progress.

Even when we face this doubt, we can take small steps towards what God has for us, empowered by the Holy Spirit. We can move in faith and continue to believe Him and take Him at His Word because we know He is always faithful to bring the harvest. He is faithful to bring fulfillment.

with a heart for harvesting

Waiting on God to fulfill His Word reminds me of Sarah and Abraham in the Bible. They were waiting on the promise of a child from God and their responses were different.

Sarah laughed and didn't believe it was possible (Genesis 17:11-12). She had even tried to devise a plan that would work when her hope to have a child hadn't been fulfilled yet out of impatience and frustration (Genesis 16:1-2).

Abraham also thought it seemed unbelievable (Genesis 17:17) but he pushed past his unbelief. He chose to take God at His word and responded by taking the action that God was calling him to by making a covenant with the Lord and obeying him immediately (Genesis 17:23).

God does keep His promise to them, just as He does with us. We have the choice to respond either by taking action and moving in faith in obedience to God or by taking matters into our own hands out of a mindset of doubt and unbelief. Our choice is to either focus on the impossibility of the situation, or to focus on the power of God.

Many of us respond in both ways. Thankfully, Jesus is ready to forgive us and extend more grace to us when we respond with doubt.

A lot of us don't want to admit the things we hope and dream for because it seems like a good way to handle them just in case they don't happen—just in case God doesn't do it. For Sarah and Abraham, that was a promise about a child. For us, it might be a promise from scripture or a personal promise God has made to us.

how much more?

God is responsible for the harvest. We plant the seeds, but He makes things grow (1 Corinthians 3:6-7). Knowing and believing that He will bring us a harvest invites us to be less afraid in pursuing our hopes and dreams because even if that harvest isn't exactly what we anticipated, we can have confidence that none of our efforts are wasted in the Kingdom of God. "Now he who supplies seed to the sower and bread for food will also supply and increase your store of seed and will enlarge the harvest of your righteousness" (2 Corinthians 9:10 NIV).

You have a dream for a reason, and you can accomplish it with the power of God. I'm not telling you to hustle. Hustling is often spinning our own wheels tirelessly, trying to make things happen in our own power like Sarah, and setting our focus on one specific desire. It's maybe even shoving aside other roles and responsibilities God might be calling us to to get to where we want to be.

God offers us a better way. He made a covenant with us, and He will keep it. We can pursue our hopes and dreams with hearts of harvesting and with God on our side.

First, we surrender. We weigh the things we want before the Lord, and we are honest and specific. Abraham asked God to include Ishmael under his blessing (Genesis 17:18). He asked for what he wanted, and he was specific, and God responded to him by saying *yes*.

Next, we need to take action. God is all powerful, and He isn't limited by what we do, but it's important to show up and show Him that what we want is worth it to us by taking some

with a heart for harvesting

initiative, maybe making some sacrifices, and ultimately doing the work He's asking us to do. Every action you take toward your dream is an expression of belief that God will accomplish it. He sees every sacrifice you make to show up, and He loves it.

If you start to doubt that you'll ever get what you want, remember you *will* reap a harvest.

God isn't a vending machine, and He isn't going to give us everything we want just because we want it. He will keep His promises to us, and one of those is that we will reap what we sow (Galatians 6:7).

The tireless work, the early mornings, the countless conversations with friends, the long commute, the outpouring of empathy, your financial sacrifice—He sees all of it. He knows all of it, and He is promising you that it isn't for nothing.

My husband is an incredibly hard worker. He goes above and beyond in every area of his life and is the classic overachiever. In one circumstance, he was working so hard. I felt like almost all of his time and attention went to this one thing, as he was spending early mornings, late nights, and weekends on it. We were confident that God would reward him for all of his hard work.

The timeframe in which we expected all of the hard work to pay off came and went, and we decided to take action. We prayerfully considered what the conversation needed to look like, and we approached it cautiously. I fully anticipated that conversation to go incredibly well and for my husband to finally be recognized for the huge investment he had made.

Instead, my husband came home defeated, angry, and confused.

If you'd been in the room with me, watching my husband come home after working so hard for over a year and realizing there was no reward in the end, you would have thought exactly what I was thinking at that moment: "It's not fair."

We made a lot of sacrifices for this. It was challenging for both of us. And there was nothing to come of it?

We felt let down, hurt, and our expectations for what hard work resulted in were disappointed.

I felt strongly in my spirit that although no one else noticed the hard work my husband had done, God did. I believed we would still reap what we had sown. I prayed for God to show us that He saw the investment we had made and that He would reward us for all of the generosity and effort.

Later that year, He did. God showed us that no investment is wasted in a personal way that became a reminder to us that He sees everything. "For the eyes of the Lord range throughout the earth to strengthen those whose hearts are fully committed to him" (2 Chronicles 16:9 NIV).

In the Bible, we are told we will reap what we sow (Galatians 6:7). This is so comforting to remember if you start to wonder if your time and effort is worth it. You get to participate by taking steps towards your dreams and hopes, and then you can entrust the miracle working to be done by God.

with a heart for harvesting

God always brings the harvest, but there is an action required—you have to sow. You have to move in obedience when God is calling you to something. You have to be willing to step out in faith and trust that when you sow into something, there will be growth.

The timing might not always look how you imagined it. Maybe you want an overnight success story, but God requires patience as you wait and prepare. You can always be confident that the harvest will come, and you should be so confident that you take obedient actions towards it.

People in your life might not see your effort, but God always does. Even if you spend your early morning hours working harder than anyone else in the world will ever know, God knows. God sees. God sees the late night patience and kindness you have with your kids. He sees you driving over an hour in traffic to see a friend. He sees you rolling out of bed earlier than you want to in order to do the thing that no one else is willing to do.

Don't stress yourself out with hustling. You don't have enough hustle to sustain the work that God wants to do through you. By the power of His Spirit, you can accomplish it.

Start sowing, and do so faithfully and diligently, and watch as God brings forth a harvest.

We can take credit for hustling, but we can't take credit for the harvest. Only a good, all powerful God can bring a harvest and multiply the effort and faithfulness in our lives that no one else

how much more?

sees.

He sees it, and He promises to reward it.

God will not let your investment in your dreams go to waste. Take obedient steps toward your God-given dreams, and He will honor those steps.

CHAPTER 20

directed to your purpose

When your desires are surrendered to God and met with His power, they can become a vision and hope for your future. They gently guide and direct you toward God and the vision and purpose He has for your life.

If you keep them tucked away and try to ignore them, they will either take you farther from God in frustration and disappointment, or they will be like a ticking time bomb, just waiting to go off and disrupt your life.

Partnering with the Holy Spirit on a journey towards the desires God has planted in us has the potential to bring us into an exciting adventure with God-one that is full of delight in God, that allows the most of God's glory into our lives, while creating the greatest impact for His kingdom.

Our lives should be filled with joy and delight no matter the circumstances because that is reflective of who God is. He wants to give you a life full of joy. It starts with those dreams and hopes for the future that you have in your heart.

how much more?

As newlyweds, my husband and I made some ambitious plans for a three day weekend. I had no experience backpacking at the time, but my husband planned this trip for us because it had been a dream of his to one day get to share this activity he loved with his wife.

We chose to explore a desert wilderness area in west Colorado that had some epic arches and really cool looking hikes. I wasn't a huge part in planning the trip because my cluelessness wouldn't have been much help.

When you backpack, you bring everything you need for the trip in a backpack. It's a pretty simple concept. We were both equipped with all of our gear, excited for a weekend away, and stoked to get outside of the office settings we were used to.

The first thing we did when we arrived at our wilderness destination was stop by the ranger station and get a paper map. I know; so retro. We needed a paper map because the lack of service wouldn't allow us to use our cell phones. We excitedly drove on a rocky, single lane road through the deserted, mountainous area, and were the only people in sight.

Because the map was black and white, it all looked the same to us, so our plan was simple: take that little dirt road until we felt like we should park, park our car somewhere off to the side, and grab our backpacks and hike around until we decide to set up camp. You might already be thinking that was a terrible idea, and you would be right because it was.

After aimlessly hiking around with our heavy backpacks for hours, in ninety degree heat, we were both dripping in sweat.

directed to your purpose

We had no idea where we were going and couldn't find a good place to set up a tent among the cacti.

We had no idea where we were going, and we both agreed this wasn't the trip we had hoped for. Even with a map in hand, we were directionless.

Hopping inside of our car sweaty and exhausted after hiking all the way back just to regroup, we slumped down, disappointed in our trip so far. This time as we looked over our map again, we came up with a plan.

The question we asked ourselves first is one that God often uses to add direction and purpose to our lives, "What do you want?"

We took a quick little inventory of our desires for our weekend backpacking. We wanted to be close to those big arches that had the epic views and hiking trails, so we found those on the map. We wanted a view from our tent, but we didn't want to be too far from our car because our backpacks were so heavy. Since we were in a desert, we had to carry all of our water with us. (Water turned out to be really heavy; who knew?)

With our new plan (and a little more sunscreen) we went back outside and tried again, and this time, we were a lot less frustrated. We were able to find a great, flat spot for our tent, near an overlook that provided an incredible view of the sun setting and rising over the desert. We were close to the hiking trails, and we had enough time to set up our tent, do all the hikes we had hoped for, and even try our first free climb together through one of those big, orange arches.

how much more?

That weekend wasn't exactly what I had pictured backpacking would look like. It wasn't the exact weekend we had had in mind, but it ended up being the perfect first backpacking trip for us, and we both look back fondly on the memories we made.

A lot of the time, I try to ignore what I want, and I end up just hiking around frustrated with my heavy backpack, sweaty and stepping on cacti. But when I give over my desires to God, tell Him what I want, and allow Him to direct me, the desires actually pull me towards Him.

The things we want can become like a map to our purpose. They can lead us toward what God has in store for us, and ultimately, that is where we will find the most joy. There will be difficult and trying seasons as believers—it isn't always going to be amazing and easy, like a walk in the park. You still might be in the desert, sleeping on rocks and carrying everything you have with you in a heavy backpack, but you will be delighted in that moment because you are delighting in God and how He is with you in your dreams and desires.

Even when your desires aren't yet fulfilled, you can find joy in who God is. He knows your desires, and He will use them to direct you toward a life with Him-a life that is full of delight in who He is and in the journey we get to adventure on with Him.

Sometimes, we start hiking without taking time to read the map. God is inviting us to take a closer look at the clues He is giving us into our purpose and into His plan. It can give you direction so you can start hiking without too much frustration, uncertainty, and ultimately disappointment. You will be

directed to your purpose

disappointed when you're confronted with what you don't want but haven't taken the time to pursue what you do want.

When we sat in the car making a plan, we were able to start moving toward it. We planned for a hike and were surprised when we ended up doing a free climb. It was more difficult than the hike we had planned for, and honestly, it wasn't something we even considered trying until we got there, but at the top, we were all smiles and high fives. It's my favorite story to tell about that trip. It never would have happened if we hadn't started by admitting we wanted to find a trailhead.

God is prepared and excited to surprise us once we get started. He wants to use some of our desires as little hints to get us going in the right direction. In His sovereign, all-knowing, and all-powerful ways, He can change our direction or course of action when He needs to. He's also ready to give us vision and direction through the things we want, when we take the time to invite God into them.

What are those dreams, desires, and hopes you have for your life? How do you think God is speaking to you through them, giving you direction, pushing you toward the trail He wants you on? If you recognize a sense of disappointment, maybe you need to look for the clues God has given you to give you direction.

CHAPTER 21

calling him Lord

Have you ever been in a season where you are repeatedly waiting for God to move, but it just isn't happening?

It can feel like you have been abandoned by God, and you're left wondering if He sees your pain, your need, and your longing for Him to move in your life and to bring renewal.

During a time like this that I experienced, I felt frustrated, far from God, and lost in disappointment. I went to a worship service at church, even though church was honestly the last place I wanted to be.

I knew God knew the circumstance and season I was in, and I was desperate for a move of God in my life. At church, as I worshiped, I spent that time continually asking God for the transformation I wanted to see in my life. I was desperate for a breakthrough and kept asking God to move. I knew He had authority over the circumstances, so I contended in prayer for Him to show up.

In my frustration, I wondered why I had to beg God to move. Have you ever felt like you were begging God? In my spirit, I felt the Holy Spirit respond to me, "You're my daughter. You

how much more?

don't have to beg me."

I had been continuously begging God for something—begging Him out of a place of desperation and need—when He wanted me to have the confidence and authority a daughter of God has. It wasn't wrong of me to ask, but the way I was asking was out of desperation and hopelessness. The posture of my heart when I approached Him lacked faith and certainty.

I needed God to move. I wanted God to move. But I didn't trust that He would. When I asked, I expected to have to ask again. In my spirit, I had already determined God wouldn't respond when I asked.

God was highlighting to me this mindset I had adopted where I felt like I needed to continually beg for things, not knowing if or when He would ever care to respond or show up. Sometimes, God brings us into seasons where we are called to be persistent in prayer. But what I felt like He wanted to show me was that He already knew what I was asking for before I even approached Him with it.

He knew my needs. He had the ability to provide. There was a difference I saw between begging from a position of unbelief and asking with confidence and faith in who God is.

Being the good God that He is, He answered my prayer that night in an incredible and miraculous way. He had wanted to get to my heart first though and shift my mindset too.

Because God is always the same, I thought what He spoke to my spirit that night had likely already been spoken before through His Word. God never changes and neither does His voice—what He speaks to us is always consistent with what we find in the Word.

This is what I found:

> *The next day, when they came down from the mountain, a large crowd met him. A man in the crowd called out, 'Teacher, I beg you to look at my son, for he is my only child. A spirit seizes him and he suddenly screams; it throws him into convulsions so that he foams at the mouth. It scarcely ever leaves him and is destroying him. I begged your disciples to drive it out, but they could not.*
> Luke 9:37-40, NIV

After this, Jesus rebukes the spirit and heals the boy, and all glory is given to God, as Jesus needs only a word to change the circumstance.

When I saw this story in my Bible, I recognized the heart of the man as he was approaching the disciples with the same posture I often approached God with. I was begging Him out of my desperation, instead of just asking, out of faith that He is the God He says He is. The difference is small, but it's important.

I started noticing Jesus' interactions with people throughout the gospels, and I saw something interesting. Jesus often invites people to ask for something specific. He is such a generous God. He's constantly inviting us to ask for more from Him, and He's always ready to give to us.

> *He called out, "Jesus Son of David, have mercy on me!"*

how much more?

Those who led the way rebuked him and told him to be quiet, but he shouted all the more, "Son of David, have mercy on me!" Jesus stopped and ordered the man to be brought to him. When he came near, Jesus asked him, "What do you want me to do for you?" "Lord, I want to see," he replied. Jesus said to him, "Receive your sight; your faith has healed you." Immediately he received his sight and followed Jesus, praising God. When all the people saw it, they also praised God."
Luke 18:38-43, NIV

Jesus knew this man wanted to see, but there was something so important about the moment when Jesus asked the man to make his desires clear to Him and to everyone who was watching. When Jesus asked this man what he wanted, he responded with, "Lord, I want to see."

He told Jesus of his desire for his sight, but first he called him Lord. This showed Jesus, and everyone else watching, that the man believed God was who He said He was. He believed Jesus was the one with authority, and he willingly put him in the place of Lord over his life.

Then, after recognizing God was who He said He was, he asked for what he wanted.

He received his sight because Jesus is all-powerful, loving, and kind, and He was able to restore this man's life by giving him the eyes he was originally designed to have.

His response was to praise God and follow Jesus, and everyone who saw it also praised God. There was a bigger picture than

calling him Lord

just giving this man his sight back—this miracle was building faith in God as the restoration happened.

In the beginning of the story, we're told, "Those who led the way rebuked him and told him to be quiet, but he shouted all the more" (Luke 18:38, NIV).

Does that voice sound familiar to you, the one telling you not to bother God with your small, silly request?

I recognize that voice because I've heard it when I try to approach God. Most often, I'm that voice in my head, *"Don't ask God to change that or to do that. It doesn't really matter. He doesn't care about that, that's such a small, silly detail."*

I've also been given a side eye when I say a prayer request that sounds straight up silly to someone else. I've been told my request is too specific and have been met with a generalization like, "We'll pray God will have His way in that circumstance."

This response doesn't reflect the confidence we can have in being loved by God. He loves us so much. He's inviting us to ask. I actually think God wants our specific requests. Mark Batterson wrote, "The more faith you have, the more specific your prayers will be. And the more specific your prayers are, the more glory God receives."[8]

God invites us to ask and to be specific. He's inviting us to call Him Lord first and submit ourselves to knowing He can do it—He can do anything—and putting our entire life before Him to use as He sees fit for His purposes.

how much more?

Jesus wasn't bothered by the man asking.

Actually, He stopped what He was doing, brought the man closer to Him, and asked him to be specific in asking for exactly what he wanted. Then He gave it to him, resulting in a huge impact when everyone responded in praising God. The glory was God's.

God wants to do that with what you want. He wants you to approach Him with the courage and boldness to ask as someone who calls Him "Lord." You can trust in knowing He is the God of all authority. When you ask boldly, you're telling Him who you believe Him to be, and you're putting Him in the position of "Lord" of your life. Asking Him as Lord reminds us of the authority He has, and it honors Him as we choose to believe He is God and He is capable.

He's asking us, "What do you want?" because when He restores and blesses us, it builds His Kingdom and gives Him glory. When we are specific in what we ask for, we give Him the opportunity to answer a prayer in a way that puts His glory on display through His specific response.

When He asks us what we want, we have the chance to respond with, "You are Lord of my life, you are in charge, and I'm asking you for this because I'm yours, and I know you can do it."

You don't have to beg Him to move in your life. When you ask boldly, Jesus is there. He stops, and He listens.

He brings you closer. He wants you face to face because what

calling him Lord

you're asking about matters to Him, and He wants you to be closer so He can focus on you even with a crowd around you.

He wants to hear your request. He wants to pull you in closer. The best part is the impact your sharing it with Him can have because people are watching.

CHAPTER 22

who is able

When I've been on a vacation for a few days, I start to think about my next vacation. Instead of thinking about going home and returning to normal life, I get the vacation blues, and I'll start to think I can get ahead of it by planning my next trip-one that's even better.

This often results in losing focus on the current memories that are being made. I start to plan far ahead instead, and get distracted. I forget to soak in the moments that are right in front of me.

God wants to give good gifts to His kids, and that often means He's going to give you something better than what you could ever imagine. What He gives us is a reflection of who He is, and He is so, so good. He wants to give you more and better things because He loves you so much.

You get to ask Him for those future dreams and plans He has for you, and sometimes, He will reveal to you what is next. But at times, He wants us to first focus on the good things that are right in front of us. God doesn't withhold good things from His children (Psalm 84:11), so, we can thank Him for things He has for us right now. It could be that the best thing for us is

how much more?

right in front of us.

He invites us to enjoy what He has already given us. He wants to do more for you than you think, but the "more" and "better" things come from stewardship and delight in the current thing.

In the New Testament, we often see Jesus asking people to be specific about what they want. He invites them to ask for healing, to ask for Him to go see their family member, to ask for food. We also see God ask people about what they want in the Old Testament. One example is when God asks Solomon to ask Him for absolutely anything.

> *That night God appeared to Solomon and said to him, "Ask for whatever you want me to give you." Solomon answered God, "You have shown great kindness to David my father and have made me king in his place. Now, Lord God, let your promise to my father David be confirmed, for you have made me king over a people who are as numerous as the dust of the earth. Give me wisdom and knowledge, that I may lead this people, for who is able to govern this great people of yours?" God said to Solomon, "Since this is your heart's desire and you have not asked for wealth, possessions or honor, nor for the death of your enemies, and since you have not asked for a long life but for wisdom and knowledge to govern my people over whom I have made you king, therefore wisdom and knowledge will be given you. And I will also give you wealth, possessions and honor, such as no king who was before you ever had and none after you will have.*
> 2 Chronicles 1:7-12, NIV

Solomon's response amazes me and convicts me every time I

who is able

read it. There is so much we can learn from his posture. God allows Solomon to ask for anything, and he responds by first recognizing and acknowledging the things God has already done. It is so easy to skip this step. It's easy to be distracted by the hope of what is next and to miss what is right in front of you or what God has already done.

Solomon asks specifically for wisdom and knowledge to guide him in the role God had already positioned him in. If I put myself in the passage, I might be asking God for a new position, for something better that I have my eye on, instead of asking Him to give me the wisdom and knowledge needed to manage what I already have.

Solomon is humbly recognizing all that God has entrusted to him already is a lot, and he needs God to be with him in this position. His question is, "Who is able to govern these great people of yours?" And I feel like I can hear him saying, "I can't do this without you, God; only you can accomplish this, and I need you to equip me for it." He is noticing God has already given him a really good thing, and he feels the weight of the responsibility in it.

God invites Solomon to ask for more, and then He gives it to him. God's response to Solomon's request is to give him what he asked for and to give him wealth, possessions, and honor, which were all things he probably wanted, yet he chose to ask for the thing that glorified God the most and served God's people the best.

Solomon asked for the thing that would empower him to be a better leader, to impact the kingdom of God, and to be a wise

how much more?

and knowledgeable leader. Then, God gave him way more than he'd ever asked for.

God is a generous God, and He has entrusted all of us with really good gifts. He wants us to first acknowledge the good things He has given us—to recognize the ways He has been at work in our lives. When He asks what we want, I hope our hearts look like Solomon's.

I hope, even as you're reflecting on what God has already done for you, that you are overwhelmed with gratitude and thanksgiving, thinking of how God has given to you so generously. And I hope you know that this season you're in right now matters.

Try asking God how you can honor Him in it. He will equip you with everything you need and even more.

When your heart is in a place to look up at God, full of thankfulness, and say, "Wow; I can't do this without you God, but I'm so honored you chose me," He can do so much more in and through you.

When you're focused on what God wants to do in and through you right where you're at, that's where He starts to invite you to ask for what you want. He will offer even more than what is asked for. He's just that good.

When we're focused and passionate about what we are partnering with God to build and create, not only in the future but also in the present, we stop looking over our shoulders wondering if there's something better out there because what

who is able

we have is the best. With God, it will prosper.

CHAPTER 23

false summits

Contentment can feel unachievable at times. It can feel far off and maybe even impossible; especially when there are so many things you want or hope for and you are living in the tension of hoping for more but not yet seeing the fullness.

There are so many tips and tricks to steer away from what you want and to focus on what God has already given. To begin your day, turn your prayer journal into a gratitude list, and pray, and praise God. This can sometimes feel like you're hiding a part of yourself from God because you are still yearning for more.

I want things in life. I want happiness, I want my family to be safe, I want my marriage to be thriving, I want our financial position to allow us to give generously, I want my career to be fulfilling, I want to have reliable and deep friends to do life with, and I want the entire dollar section at Target.

I also want to see the Kingdom of God invade the earth, and I want to be a part of it. I want to watch lives get transformed before my eyes. I want the church to be more of a safe place, less of a social club, and I want desperate people to find a home. (A lot of times, I'm one of the desperate people looking for one).

how much more?

If you were with me in the morning when I wake, you would see me shuffling out of bed over to the kitchen in my slippers to make some coffee. You'd watch me brew way too much coffee for one person to drink. Then, I'd quietly tiptoe past my puppy who would certainly perk up in her bed and make eye contact, but she would know I'm not taking her outside yet, so staying cuddled up is her best move.

With a coffee cup in hand, I would sit on our blue, mid-century, modern couch and open my Bible, the living word of God. I do this every day. Even on vacation, even when I'm busy, even— or maybe especially—when God feels far, far away.

If you were there, you'd see the morning light shifting through the window as the sun rose, and you'd watch me sip my coffee, read over the Word, and get out a journal to scribble down a few things.

From the outside, it looks like nothing has happened. It looks like a typical morning routine. It looks as though when I get up from that couch and go about my day, there is nothing different about me or my circumstances. But that wouldn't be the truth.

Everything changes the moment you go to God, in an act of surrender, and hand Him all of your dreams and desires. Everything changes when He pulls you close, and meets you with everything you need. Everything changes when He takes your surrender and turns it into satisfaction. He fills you with contentment while still promising you more.

Contentment is not just in receiving from God, just in asking of God or giving to God. It's all of those things.

false summits

Sometimes, it's falling on my knees giving to God what I know I cannot carry and asking for Him to come.

Other times, it's showing up day after day, asking for the same thing, but standing up without seeing the promise yet and moving in trust, confident that I can still show up and ask again tomorrow.

When hiking a 14er (a 14,000 foot mountain), you often have to begin the hike in the dark.
We hiked the tallest 14er in the state of Colorado, Mt. Elbert, and we began this hike in total darkness around 4 a.m. It's a weird but beautiful journey on these hikes. All you can really do is take the next step, follow the path, and hope you end up on top of a mountain. And that's all you do—you just keep taking that next step—for hours. That persistence of just taking the next step is a lot like what my walk with God feels like. It might sound familiar to you too.

There isn't a map or cell phone service, and the hikes are long. The mountains can be ruthless, and you don't want to be on top of a 14,000 foot mountain when an afternoon storm starts to roll in because the weather at higher altitudes changes quickly. From the start, you may not even be able to see the peak you're trying to reach. I often feel like I'm trying to reach something I cannot even see when I'm moving toward what God has called me to.

We started this hike just watching our feet with a headlamp, and then slowly, the sun began to rise, and we kept on stepping. With or without sunlight, you just watch your feet and take that next step.

how much more?

Eventually, when you're above the treeline, you might start to make assumptions about the path based on what you can see. It feels like you can see the top and when you can see it, you feel so close. There's the place where the sky gets interrupted by the massive structure of the mountain, and that's where you're heading. You'll start to hear or say to yourself, "There's the peak! We're almost there. I can see it!"

But often, with these mountains, and with Mt. Elbert, there's something called a "false summit." Essentially, it's a peak of a mountain that appears to be the top of the mountain, but once you get there, there are higher peaks, and you're hours away from the real summit. In my walk with God, there have been so many times when I thought, "if I just make it there, then I'll have made it."

On Mt. Elbert, this happens multiple times. You get so high up, your lungs are struggling to breathe, and your muscles aren't getting enough oxygen, but you just keep stepping. It can feel discouraging and maybe even impossible, but to succeed, all you have to do is keep moving.

When I picture my walk with God, I often picture it like this experience. Sometimes, it feels like you're in the dark at the trailhead. You know there's a mountain in front of you, you can sense how huge it is, but all you can do is get on the trail.

You don't see the peak yet, there might be false summits, and your limited knowledge is only of the trail immediately in front of you.

You know there is a mountaintop, a future, a hope. You know

false summits

that dream you have, that hope you have, you can sense that it is somewhere in front of you. You don't know what the path will look like until you're on it. So, you just get on your way. It's the only thing you know how to do.

You know those specific things that you feel called to by God, yet at times you might doubt them, wondering if you really hear God. There might be times when it feels like you can see the peak and think you're almost there. And there might be times when you feel like you are watching your feet with a headlamp and have no knowledge of what is ahead of you.

With God, we can be content in knowing He is the One who calls us. He's the One who set your feet on the trail, put the dream in your heart, and He will accomplish it. You don't have to do it on your own strength. You don't have to "figure it out" or push through by will power or self-reliance.

You can just walk into that foggy picture of the hope you have for the future you're called to, even if it feels too early and it's 4 a.m. Maybe you feel tired, groggy, unprepared, or uncertain, but you can still take your first step and then just stay persistent in stepping.

Know that He is right there with you, at the base of the mountain in the dark, and on the trail when the treeline disappears and the oxygen thins. He's with you at every false summit, pushing you to keep moving, and He's at the top when you finally see the view from the summit.

You don't have to be certain of what the end looks like, but you need to be certain of who is with you on the journey.

how much more?

When you know Him and know His voice, you can be confident He will accomplish all that He said He would. When you are certain of His faithfulness, even when the path isn't clear, you know He is leading you and directing each step.

What comes next? I don't know. But I know a God who does, and that's enough. That's contentment.

There's still a lot of mystery, but when we release and surrender the unknowns and uncertainty to God, who we can be certain of, we find contentment. No matter what position you find yourself in on the journey, you can be content, not because of the position, but because of who is guiding you on the trail.

He is faithful. He keeps His promises. He knows what's next, and He's got it. Let's just be faithful to be persistent, continuing to move forward toward the mountain.

CHAPTER 24

I'm ready

You might have heard the prayer "Not my will, but yours." This prayer is taken from Scripture. It's taken from a pivotal moment in the gospel message where Jesus, the Son of God, prays to His Father before He is crucified.

Jesus is fully God, so He didn't need to pray to God. He is God, and He is all-knowing. So, why He did this seems simple: He did it for us.

He prayed so we would know how to pray—He gave us a specific example of what it looks like to turn to God.

When I read this story, I see how human Jesus positioned Himself to be in that moment, and I thank God He sent His son to know and understand the depths of the mess that is the human heart. If you're ever asking yourself if someone understands, I can assure you; Jesus does.

Jesus shared this intimate conversation with His Father in the Garden of Gethsemane. But I can't help but be reminded of a pair that was in another garden in the beginning of the story. Adam and Eve also found themselves in a garden, and they were facing a choice.

how much more?

Adam and Eve had a desire. There was something else they wanted aside from what God had already given them. Their desire was grown in them by the enemy who tempted them to fulfill that desire in their own timing and in their own way.

"Just take one bite," he said, "and then you will be content. God is withholding something good from you. He doesn't want you to have it, but you can take it into your own hands and take it for yourself." He caused them to question what God had really said.

Have you ever heard that voice in your head before? I have, and I don't blame them for believing it.

They wanted to know more. What they wanted didn't seem evil. It didn't seem wrong or bad to simply want more knowledge. Who wouldn't want that? Isn't that a good thing?

Why wouldn't God want that for them? Why was God withholding something good from them? Didn't they deserve good things?

So, they ate the fruit, and the results were destructive.

Their focus had been on the one thing God had said "no" to, instead of the abundance all around them that God had already provided and said "yes" to. Sometimes, you might become focused on the one thing that you really want, the thing that God seems to not be paying attention to, when maybe you need to shift your eyes and look around at what He has already given you.

I'm ready

In the garden of Gethsemane, Jesus is praying to His Father, and it's because He *doesn't* want something. It is still all about desire, but His desire looks different.

In the message translation, it reads like this: "Going a little ahead, he fell on his face, praying, 'My Father, if there is any way, get me out of this. But please, not what I want. You, what do you want?'" (Matthew 26:39, MSG).

The difference between Adam and Eve in the garden versus Jesus in the garden is in how they respond.

They all had things they wanted or didn't want, and so do we. Adam and Eve took hold of their desires and believed the lie that they had to take this good thing they wanted because God wouldn't give it to them. Then, when the results were disastrous, they hid. They went and tried to hide from God both the thing that they wanted that drove them to the action and the action itself. Their response created space between them and God.

Jesus also had something He wanted. He took that desire, He fell on His face, and He prayed. He told the Lord He didn't want it. He went to God and He said, "I don't want this. But what do you want?"

And our good, all-powerful God transformed.

In verse 42, Jesus' disposition changes. You can see it in the text when He declares, "I'm ready. Do it your way."

I don't think Jesus' desire went away. I don't think He watched

how much more?

the desire magically get sent up to Heaven in the little tube you use at the drive thru window at the bank.

God brought revelation. God revealed Himself, His plan, and His purpose to Jesus when Jesus went to Him, and that gave Jesus the ability to want what God wanted more than what He wanted. The Father brought both transformation and fulfillment when Jesus went to Him.

That's what God wants for you, too.

The question "what do you want?" is the question Jesus asked the blind man, showing us we are invited to answer this question. It's also the same question He asked God in the garden, demonstrating to us to ask God, "what do you want?"

I don't think God wants us to hear those lies whispered in our ears, to take matters into our own hands, and then to hide because something we wanted didn't seem wrong but took us to a place that left us feeling like we needed to hide from God.

I don't think God wants the things we want to push us further from Him. He wants to use them to draw us closer.

He wants us to follow the example Jesus gave us.

You will want things. You probably already have more than one dream or hope that you are continually reminded of as you read this book. It's actually a good thing, and it can be incredibly powerful when we let God fulfill our desires with His plans, purpose and person.

I'm ready

Take your dreams, your hopes, your desires and fall to your knees. Go to your garden or your favorite reading chair, your meeting place with God. Tell God what you want, what you don't want, and what you don't understand. He offers both transformation and fulfillment. Jesus said: "Whoever drinks the water I give them will never thirst. Indeed, the water I give them will become in them a spring of water welling up to eternal life" (John 4:14, NIV).

Ask Him what He wants. Ask Him for His plans for you. Invite Him to allow His hopes and dreams for you to well up. Let Him do the powerful, transformative work in you so you can stand up with confidence and contentment saying, "I'm ready. Do it your way."

It will change you.

I want you to live a life of abundance, full of the power of God. I also want you to change the world. Jesus stood up and did something that made no sense to anyone else, and well, we're still talking about it today. It started with a moment alone with the Father. Then, the change Jesus experienced led Him to change the world.

People were standing at the foot of the cross wondering why Jesus refused to take matters into His own hands. There was no way He wanted this. No one wants to die a brutal death on a cross. So if He could just hop off the cross, then why didn't He?

Because He knew who His Father was.

how much more?

He knew who was really in charge in that moment, and He genuinely wanted what God wanted in that moment more than what He wanted.

By the power of His Spirit, we can want what God wants too. Even if it's hard, and even if it hurts, you can go out in the world on your unique assignment saying, "I'm ready; do it your way," because you know who your Father is.

Jesus' desire paired with the power of God led Him to fulfill His purpose.

Jesus' desire took Him to the intimate and memorable place in the garden where He cried out to God.

What He didn't want drove Him not farther from God, but closer to Him. When God met Him in that place, together they fulfilled the purpose for Jesus' life. They changed the world.

Your hopes and dreams, met with the power of God, can change the world too.

You have options. You can hide the things you want. You can try to forget about them. You can deem them as unimportant or categorize them as something that will probably never happen. You can throw up your hands saying, "It doesn't matter," or "It's impossible."

Or, you can take them to God. In an intimate meeting, God can shift and move your desires into alignment with His.

Be ready to answer the question "what do you want?" and be

I'm ready

willing to ask the Father the same question.

This is where you will see promises fulfilled. This is where you will live in your purpose and in contentment. This is when you start to see the world become transformed.

I'm ready, God. Do it your way.

notes

1. Willard, Dallas. 2012 Renovation of the Heart: Putting on the Character of Christ. Colorado Springs, CO: Navpress.

2. L'Engle, Madeleine. 1980, 1998, 2001. New York, New York: Convergent Books.

3. Piper, John. When I Don't Desire God: How to Fight for Joy: Study Guide

4. Ortberg, John. 2014. Soul Keeping. Grand Rapids, Michigan: Zondervan.

5. Acuff, Jon. 2013. Start. Brentwood, TN: Lampo Press.

6. Oliver, Mary. 2016. Upstream. New York, New York: Penguin Press.

7. Willard, Dallas. 2012 Renovation of the Heart: Putting on the Character of Christ. Colorado Springs, CO: Navpress.

8. Batterson, Mark. 2011. The Circle Maker. Grand Rapids, Michigan: Zondervan.

acknowledgements

To the UHP team: Thank you for believing in faith with me that this message matters. Your prayers, insight, and practical assistance took this book from an idea floating around in my head to something that can be put on a bookshelf.

To my Threshold community: Thank you for being my first readers! Your devotion to showing up to hear from God continually motivates and challenges me. Thank you for being faithful believers in my big, crazy dreams and for pursuing your own.

To my writing & coaching community: The writing life is a weird, wild journey and I'm forever grateful I don't have to do it alone. Collaborating with some of the most incredible creatives chasing after God-given dreams is a true honor. You inspire me.

To my prayer warriors (you know who you are!): Thank you for being the kind of people to send voice texts of prophetic words when I can't see the finish line. Thank you for chasing after God's vision for your lives, and for the lives of those around you. I know your prayers and visions have carried me through. I believe you quite literally prayed this into existence.

To my husband: You're the only one who has truly seen the struggle, persistence, and commitment this dream required. Thank you for never calling me crazy, for always being there to hold my hand, and for saying you believed I'd be a bestselling author before I even had a blog. Without you, I would have forgotten to eat dinner a lot of times, and this book would have never been written. Thank you for reading a thousand terrible first drafts and for increasing the coffee budget. Love you forever.

about the author

Molly Wilcox is an author and coach. She has an English degree from Taylor University and has been featured on Bible Gateway, Darling Magazine, Grit & Virtue, and Way Media. She was also a contributing writer for The Abide Bible. Her weekly newsletter "Threshold: Entering into a Holy Place" invites others to take a step toward transforming their mundane moments into holy ones.

As a certified Hope*Writers coach, she empowers faithful creatives to chase after their God-given dreams. When she isn't writing, reading, or coaching, she's probably showing a stranger pictures of her mini goldendoodle pup.

She lives with her husband in Franklin, TN.

Social Media Handles:
@MrsMollyWilcox (Instagram, Pinterest, TikTok)
Website: MrsMollyWilcox.com

www.ingramcontent.com/pod-product-compliance
Lightning Source LLC
Chambersburg PA
CBHW030324100526
44592CB00010B/561